Praise For
When Your Aging Parent Needs Help

"With its handy checklists ('downloadable cheatsheets') and illuminating vignettes ('What This Looks Like'), this book is a terrific guide for families starting on their caregiving journey. The exhortations to focus on the patient's perspective and the gentle reminders that caregiving is often frustratingly difficult make the manual especially valuable."

> —*Muriel R. Gillick, MD*
> *Harvard Medical School, author of The Caregiver's Encyclopedia: A Compassionate Guide to Caring for Older Adults*

"An essential step-by-step guide for families wondering how to respond when an older parent begins to experience difficulties. Full of sound practical advice, compassion, expert wisdom, and helpful resources."

> —*Judith Graham*
> *Navigating Aging columnist, Kaiser Health News*

"Far too many adult children struggle with uncertainty and doubt when it comes to helping their parents. This book is the missing piece that turns a puzzle into a picture."

> —*Bill Thomas, MD*
> *Founder, Changing Aging and The Eden Alternative*

"Gives adult children easy-to-understand answers to the many challenging questions they have about their aging parents' health, behavior, and safety. Even more important, it raises questions that they may not have even known to ask. And the answers are supported by communication tools and strategies to deal with obstacles they may encounter. Dr. Leslie Kernisan, a geriatrician, and her coauthor, Paula Spencer Scott, have combined their years of experience to offer practical, realistic, and respectful ways to guide both readers new to caregiving and those who are experienced but still searching."

—*Carol Levine*
Senior fellow and former director, Families and Health Care Project, United Hospital Fund, and MacArthur Foundation fellow

"An outstanding guide for anyone concerned about an aging parent. The 'cheatsheets' alone are worth ten times the purchase price, helping to ensure the best chance at success. Family caregivers stress about 'fixing' things. This guide will provide a step-by-step process for the journey."

—*Linda Fodrini-Johnson, MA, MFT, CMC*
Geriatric care manager/consultant/educator and past president, Aging Life Care Association

"As a health activist for 12 years, I've learned to watch for deep understanding and pragmatic structured tools. As an aging boomer, I hunger for compassionate guidance—for my whole family. This is a home run on both counts."

—*Dave DeBronkart*
e-Patient Dave blogger and author of Let Patients Help

"This book is a resource not just for the sons and daughters of aging parents but anyone who has to help older adults who are beginning to show signs of memory loss. Using a step-by-step process and applying them to two fictional cases, the authors give the readers practical advice on how to investigate and talk to older adults about their concerns and a clear process on how to develop realistic solutions that align with the hopes of both children and parents alike."

—*Eric Widera, MD*
Geriatrics professor, UCSF School of Medicine

"I can think of no one, and I mean no one, I would trust more than Dr. Kernisan to deliver a highly practical, understandable, and usable guide for navigating this life phase with your parents. This is a much-needed resource that I recommend for everyone, including adult children and their aging parents."

—*Anne Tumlinson*
Daughterhood.org

"Finally, a practical guide for the adult children of aging parents to help them help their parents navigate physical and cognitive decline of old age. An indispensable guide to one of the hardest things that most of us will have to do."

—*Sei Lee, MD*
Geriatrics professor, UCSF School of Medicine

"When is a memory lapse, fall, mood, or behavior change a sign of dementia versus a side effect of a medication or even a sign of an infection? How do I bring it up without scaring them or making them angry? And what do their doctors need to know? How to balance safety and independence? This is an invaluable resource to help people navigate what is too often a frightening and confusing process to ensure people get the right care."

—*Geri Lynn Baumblatt*
Family caregiver advocate and cofounder of the Difference Collaborative

"Pure gold! Whether you're planning future care for your parents or are stuck for answers about what comes next, this is your resource. Stellar advice from the doctor we all wish our parents could have."

—*Carol Bradley Bursack*
Author of Minding Our Elders

"A much-needed book that gives clear, actionable, and medically sound advice to those of us whose parents have started to need help. This book breaks down what is often an emotionally complex and daunting process into manageable steps, providing you with a road map and the tools you need to navigate the process and reassuring you along the way. I know that many will benefit from it."

—*Roy Remer*
Executive director, Zen Caregiving Project

"This book is GPS for the children of older adults. If you are caring for an aging parent, this invaluable guide will help keep you on the right road. "

—*Howard Gleckman*
Forbes columnist and author of Caring for Our Parents

"This book puts practical, useful information from a practicing geriatrician at your fingertips."

—*Alex Smith, MD*
Associate professor, UCSF School of Medicine

"A thorough exploration of the conversations, resources, checklists, and helpful hints on how to best care for aging parents. The expert insights on what to know and how to be empathetic about getting older make this an essential book."

—*Sherri Snelling*
Gerontologist, CEO of The Caregiver Club

"Dr. Kernisan and Paula Scott show us how to get started when we are worried about our parents, offering clear, pragmatic guidance and ways to handle even the thorniest of issues like dementia or our parents' resistance to help. No one is prepared for the journey, but stop worrying, read this book and get started. You are not alone."

—*Janet Simpson Benvenuti*
Founder, Circle of Life Partners and author of Don't Give Up on Me!

"Invaluable advice and direct access to practical tools—like having your own geriatrician."

—*Amy Goyer*
Family caregiving consultant and author of AARP's Juggling Work, Life, and Caregiving

When Your Aging Parent Needs Help

A geriatrician's step-by-step guide to memory loss, resistance, safety worries, and more

Leslie Kernisan, MD, MPH
Paula Spencer Scott

A Better Health While Aging Quick Book

Published in the United States by Better Health While Aging, San Francisco
hello@betterhealthwhileaging.net
1st edition

ISBN: 978-1-7361532-0-8 (print)
ISBN: 978-1-7361532-1-5 (ebook)

Cover design by Margaret Spencer

Ordering Information:
Special discounts are available on quantity purchases by corporations, associations, and others. For details, contact hello@betterhealthwhileaging.net

This book is dedicated to everyone supporting an aging parent's well-being, whether you're just starting out or deep in the journey. Your efforts and care matter and are so valuable. Even if your aging parent can't quite see it, we see it and thank you for it.

When Your Aging Parent Needs Help

A geriatrician's step-by-step
guide to memory loss, resistance,
safety worries, and more

Leslie Kernisan, MD, MPH
Paula Spencer Scott

A Better Health While Aging Quick Book

CONTENTS

Introduction

We call it the big *uh-oh:* You're concerned about your older parent and unsure what to do next. It can dawn slowly or happen fast with a single life-changing event. No matter how the awareness hits you, you sense that if you don't act quickly, in the right way, things might go very wrong.

But what can, and should, you do? And how?

Is your mom or dad still safe living alone? Is their bad driving putting others at risk? Is it just forgetfulness, or could it be Alzheimer's? Why won't they listen to your suggestions?

We can help. Dr. K is a geriatrician (a medical doctor specializing in the care of older adults) who has experience as a clinician, educator, and founder of Better Health While Aging, a popular website about aging health and eldercare. Paula is the author of *Surviving Alzheimer's: Practical Tips and Soul-Saving Wisdom for Caregivers* and leads workshops for family caregivers. Together, we've helped thousands of adult children just like you, at a similar juncture. And we've been there ourselves.

We know the uncertainty and stress, the roadblocks and landmines.

We'll show you a straightforward process that's worked for the families we've helped, a process that can turn your concerns into practical action and peace of mind.

This book is for you if...

- You've noticed memory changes in your parent, like increasing forgetfulness, repeating comments or questions, relying more on notes and reminders, missing appointments, "losing" things or getting lost in familiar places.

- Or you're seeing other kinds of thinking problems, like difficulty paying bills or keeping the house in order, or confusion about dates, time, places, or people.

- Or you're concerned about uncharacteristic choices your parent is making about money, driving, healthcare, relationships, or another big issue.

- Or your parent seems more withdrawn, apathetic, distracted, anxious, paranoid, or otherwise altered and it's affecting their activities, social life, work, or everyday functioning.

- Or you've made suggestions about these types of concerns only to have them rebuffed—either by one or both of your parents ("We're fine," "I don't want to talk about it") or another relative, like a sibling ("They're just slowing down." "Stop stirring up trouble.").

- Or not only is your help being resisted but as far as you can tell, your parent isn't getting checked out by the doctor and nobody else is being allowed to help either.

You're not only worried—you're stumped about what to do next.

People in these very situations have posted to Better Health While Aging for years, asking for help. The effective process that Dr. K has developed for the families who consult with her has never fit neatly into a short comment response, nor even an article. That's what sparked us to write this book.

We'll walk you through that process, step by step. We'll provide you with lots of practical and actionable tools, tips, worksheets, checklists, and other resources, like examples of what to say in critical situations and where to find added help. You can also follow examples that show the process in real-world situations.

We'll give you the practical advice you need—from decision-making strategies to important medical and legal concepts to insights on aging, family dynamics, and communication—to turn good intentions into workable solutions.

And because your own health and well-being are just as important as your parent's, you'll find a strong emphasis on how to balance what's ideal and what's realistic and how to best prepare yourself for the longer haul.

Let's face it, the journey of helping an older parent can be gratifying but it can also be demanding and stressful.

Having a plan for that support can, by itself, lessen some of the burden.

This book is that important first step. Congratulations for caring enough to take it.

How to Use This Book

We'd like to point out some features we've built into this book to help you along the way:

TOOLS

To help you put suggestions into action, you'll see exercises, examples, and lists throughout the text, each flagged by the word "Tool." We created them to help you tailor the advice in the text to your specific situation.

DOWNLOADABLE CHEATSHEETS

For many of the tools and other information within the book, we provide related "cheatsheets"—quick summaries or fill-in-the-blank pages that you can download and, if you like, print. Some you might want to use as worksheets—others you could bring with you to a doctor appointment. Like Tools, these are highlighted within the text. In the RESOURCES section at the end of the book, we provide a link to the book's Online Resource Center on Dr. K's website, Better Health While Aging, where you can access up-to-date versions of all the cheat-sheets.

OTHER FORMS OF HELP

Throughout the book we also refer to articles, websites, books, and other resource materials. Many of these articles live on Dr. K's website, Better Health While Aging. A complete list, with links, appears in the RESOURCES section, found at the end of the book.

"WHAT THIS LOOKS LIKE" FAMILY STORIES

Finally, to show you what the step-by-step process outlined in this book looks like in action, we'll walk you through the stories of two fictional families, the Smiths and the Johnsons. Look for the sections at the end of each chapter called "What This Looks Like."

Let's meet the Smiths and the Johnsons now:

Example 1: The Smiths

Albert Smith, 88, lives alone and is proud of his independence. He takes medication only for high blood pressure and arthritis, which haven't slowed him down. His three children live in different states. They know that in the past two years, he's had several fender benders. He also broke his wrist (they took turns briefly visiting to help him after that) and has fallen a couple of times, bruising his hip and face.

On one of those visits, his oldest son, Zeke, noticed an unpaid traffic ticket and some overdue bills. This surprised him because Albert has always been very organized. When asked about it, Albert claimed they were all mistakes by the billers and didn't remember getting any tickets. Zeke has noticed over the past year that his father seems to repeat himself but gets upset if anyone points that out. He and his younger siblings have never really talked about this.

Because of his tendency to be on top of things, Albert, years ago, assigned Zeke durable power of attorney (DPOA) and durable power of attorney for healthcare, both of the type known as springing. (We'll describe these documents in later chapters.) But they haven't talked about it since.

Lately, every time the phone rings, though, the siblings worry there's a new crisis.

Example 2: The Johnsons

Maria Johnson, a 75-year-old recent widow, also lives alone but in the same town as her only child, Sue, who sees her often. Sue is aware of increasing forgetfulness and disarray in her mother's once-tidy, well-organized house—worse since her father's death nine months ago.

She's taken to bringing Maria dinner and tries to throw away mounting clutter when she can. Increasingly, she finds spoiled food in the fridge. Once, a pot was burning on the stove when Sue walked in. Her mother also complains about how much things cost and how hard it is to keep track of all her payments. But she refuses any help. Likewise, Sue's suggestion of a medical checkup to see if anything's wrong is completely rejected. Maria has a famous dislike of doctors and doesn't seem ill otherwise. "I guess I'm just grieving," she says. "I'll be fine soon."

Sue, who works fulltime, is finding it hard to micromanage her mother's life. She doesn't have any power of attorney. She worries things are getting worse fast.

PART ONE: TAKING STOCK

Why We Always Start Here, Gathering Key Information

We get it: you want to jump in and *make it better*.

To get good results, though, it pays to understand just what's going on and how your parent sees things. Sometimes our starting assumptions are wrong. You might be seeing only part of the story. And without a clear review of the situation, it's easy to waste time and trouble or even alienate your parent, no matter how well intentioned you are. So whether you think you know where to begin or have no idea, the starting place is always the same. Step back.

Trust us: The best beginning to handling any concern about an aging parent (cognitive or otherwise) is to first clarify the problem. The specific information-gathering steps we'll describe may not feel like active problem solving. But that's what you'll be doing.

In Chapter 1, we show you how to quickly assess thinking skills, safety, life skills, and more in a well-rounded way. This is essential to confirming (or sometimes calming) initial worries, putting them in a context and giving a clearer sense of what the underlying needs are. Chapter 2 adds one big, often-overlooked dimension: Getting your parent's perspective. Whether they're communicative or resistant, whether they're aware of changes or oblivious (or seem odd or irrational about what's going on with them)—even if they completely dismiss you—this is a super productive step. It fosters goodwill and provides critical information. When you know more about how your parent sees things, you'll be better equipped to choose a course of action and to get them to go along with it.

All this deliberate setup guides your next steps—and boosts your odds for success.

Chapter 1:
Get the Facts on the Situation

Maybe you think you know exactly what the problem is and you might be right. Maybe you have only some suspicions (or frustrations) without being entirely sure what's going on. Or you might have tried to step in—either after a crisis or gradually, over time—only to have your good intentions ignored or waved away.

Wherever the situation, try to resist the understandable itch to jump in and fix it *today*.

To improve your odds of helping your parent effectively, you'll want to first run through a quick but thorough review that will help you assess just what the problems are.

You'll need to act a bit like a detective: Gathering information and talking to key players. This will put you in a better position to later consider your options and plan your next steps.

Starting this way also allows you:

- To decide whether you really need to act right now or can watch-and-wait.

- To move from vague worries to specific issues that you can problem-solve or bring to the attention of professionals.

- To find out what others have observed, which usually gives a rounder picture of things.

- To learn what family members and other key players in your family think because they're part of this, too, and are best brought in early.

- To document changes you're seeing, which will be useful in measuring any deterioration (or improvement) over time and in communicating with doctors, family members, and others. This can also be useful down the line if there's any concern about legal activity (like selling a house, changing a legal document) or financial exploitation, or if the courts get involved. (Even if this doesn't sound relevant to you now...you never know.)

- To, above all, wind up with solutions that are effective because they address the *right* needs in a *respectful* way.

We'll show you how to gather the info you'll need.

Before we go any further, though, let's name the elephant in the room: the common concern that your parent might be slipping mentally and therefore is doing things that they wouldn't if they were in good cognitive health, and that those choices are unsafe for their physical, emotional, and/or financial well-being.

This concern lies at the heart of most adult children's impulse to *Do Something*.

Some of you may be wondering if this could be "Alzheimer's" or "dementia." That's a legitimate concern, given that about one in five adults over 65 have mild cognitive impairment, a form of deterioration in how the brain manages memory, thinking, and other mental processes that doesn't necessarily impair everyday function but can be noticed by friends and family. Some cognitive impairment, though not all, progresses to dementia. (Dementia is a term used to describe a syndrome of progressive mental decline that's bad enough to interfere with daily life. For a list of types, one of which is Alzheimer's, as well as some types of cognitive decline that are reversible, see RESOURCES.)

You may very well be dealing with some level of cognitive impairment. It's often at the beginning of someone needing more help. Or there may be another issue at work.

That's all the more reason to begin by getting a sense of what's going on.

There are four basic steps:

1. **Check for worrisome signs that could indicate real memory and thinking problems.**

2. **Check for signs of problems with life tasks and safety.**

3. **Talk to family members and other "informants."**

4. **Double-check to see if any "red flag" safety issues are present.**

Let's look at each.

Step 1: Check for Worrisome Signs That Could Indicate Real Memory and Thinking Problems

Almost everyone experiences brain changes as they age, just as they experience other physical changes. (You might have already experienced "tip of the tongue syndrome" yourself, where a word is…just…out…of…reach.) When should you worry?

Certain brain changes are more worrisome than others. Here's Dr. K's list, based on what geriatricians usually ask about when checking for concerning cognitive symptoms. The first eight items are based on the "AD-8 informant interview" (a brief measure widely used in the medical community). Research has found that when it comes to detecting possible Alzheimer's, asking family members about the presence or absence of these eight particular behaviors can be just as effective as certain office-based cognitive tests. Then we list seven additional signs and symptoms that are also linked to cognitive impairment and are good to document and later report to a health provider.

TOOL AND DOWNLOADABLE CHEATSHEET: COGNITIVE SYMPTOM CHECKER

You can find a link to a downloadable cheatsheet, "Cognitive Symptom Checker," to use for this exercise at the end of the book in RESOURCES.

For each of the following eight items, think about whether you've noticed...

- A change from how your parent has typically been in the past. (If your parent has always been absentminded or bad with money, that's not as relevant as if this is new behavior.)

- Issues that seem related to thinking ability, rather than related to physical limitations (like pain, shortness of breath, a chronic ailment, or other physical disability).

If any item(s) seems to apply to your parent, write it down, along with:

- When you first noticed the problem.

- Specifics about what you've observed.

Have you noticed...

1. **Signs of poor judgment?** This means behaviors or situations that suggest bad or inappropriate decisions. Examples: worrisome spending or giving away money, making driving mistakes, choosing inappropriate clothes or wearing the same ones over and over, or not noticing a safety issue that others are concerned about (heat turned on much too high, trying to cross a busy road on foot, driving despite poor vision).

2. **Reduced interest in leisure activities?** This means being less interested and involved in one's usual favorite hobbies and ac-

tivities (like volunteering, seeing friends, club meetings, walking, sports, reading, writing). You should especially pay attention if there isn't a physical health issue interfering with doing the activity.

3. **Repeating oneself?** Has your parent started repeating questions, comments, or stories more than he or she used to?

4. **Difficulty learning to use something new?** Common examples include having trouble with a new kitchen appliance or gadget. This can be a tricky one, given that gadgets become more complicated every year. But if you've noticed anything, including difficulty operating something that was previously not a problem, like a microwave or phone, jot it down.

5. **Forgetting the year or month?** Especially once one stops working, it can be easy to lose track of the date or day of the week. But if you notice your parent forgetting the year or month, make a note of this.

6. **Difficulty managing money and finances?** Common examples include having trouble paying bills on time, struggling to balance the checkbook or add columns of numbers, or otherwise having more difficulty than one used to have relating to financial transactions. You may find unpaid bill notices or see your parent having trouble using an ATM card or making change.

7. **Problems with appointments and commitments?** Is your parent having more trouble keeping track of appointments and plans? For example, you might observe missed meetings or other engagements, notice unfilled medication refills, or see an increased reliance on memory assists like notes and Post-its.

8. **Daily struggles with memory or thinking?** It's normal for older adults to take a little longer to remember things, since many brain functions do slow a bit with aging. But if it seems that your parent often can't remember things that happened,

struggles to follow directions (such as in a recipe), often forgets common words, or otherwise seems to be more confused with thinking, make note of this.

Seeing even one of the concerning signs suggests that you're right to wonder; it's likely there's something going on that warrants being checked out.

Other Concerning Signs

In addition, the following behaviors may be relevant, as they can be related to cognitive decline and changes in mental function.

Have you noticed...

1. **Marked changes in mood and personality?** It's normal for anyone to be irritable when your routine is disrupted or things don't go as planned. More concerning is an increased tendency to become confused, suspicious, depressed, fearful, anxious, or easily upset when out of one's comfort zone or over-stressed.

2. **Increasing paranoia or suspicious thoughts?** If you've found yourself thinking your parent seems to be getting more paranoid, and this is a change from usual behavior, that would also count as a worrisome change to note. Paranoia can appear as unfounded jealousy or suspicion, or as having other unreasonable fears or irrational beliefs.

3. **A new friendship that seems to be keeping your parent away from family or old friends?** This could be innocent but is a common sign of scamming in older adults, especially if judgment and other thinking skills are impaired—the new friend may be aware of this and "moving in" on them.

4. **Recurring hallucinations?** Your parent may see people, animals, or other things that aren't there. These visual hallucinations can be frightening or friendly. Some people hallucinate smells, sounds, or touches.

5. **Movement problems?** Tremors, rigid muscles, and a shuffling walk are neurological changes that are sometimes described as "Parkinsonism." (They are not always caused by true Parkinson's disease.) These movement problems can be related to thinking changes.

6. **Loss of inhibition or tact?** Socially inappropriate behavior, making rude or offensive (or otherwise thoughtless) comments, disrobing in public, or other antisocial behaviors can be caused by changes in brain function. There's usually a lack of awareness of these changes.

7. **Obsessive or repetitive behavior?** Examples include repeatedly shaving, hoarding items, overeating, repeating words or phrases, and pacing.

If you need more help deciding whether something is a typical age-related change or more concerning, we have a link to some helpful articles in RESOURCES at the end of this book. These include a list of early signs from the Alzheimer's Association and Dr. K's article "How memory and thinking change with normal aging." These links are also provided on the Cognitive Symptom Checker cheatsheet.

Step 2: Check for Signs of Problems with Life Tasks and Safety

You'll also want to check how things are playing out in your parents' everyday lives. In addition to the brain health and mood considerations above, there are five key areas of health and well-being to consider in older adults: life tasks, safety, physical health, mood/brain health, and medication safety/management.

Life tasks refer to fundamental self-care activities we either do for ourselves or need someone to do for us. (You may hear a provider refer to this as "assessing function.")

Professionals usually categorize these tasks in two ways: Activities of

Daily Living (ADLs) are things we learn as very young children, such as walking, self-feeding, dressing, toileting, and bathing. Instrumental Activities of Daily Living (IADLs) are self-care tasks that require higher-order thinking skills and which we usually learn as teenagers, such as managing finances or medication, driving, and housecleaning.

Safety tends to be a top priority for families. Identifying specific safety concerns can help you shape practical actions to resolve them. But be aware that while older adults tend to be concerned as well, they're often willing to trade safety for autonomy and independence, which enhance their quality of life.

Bear in mind that many safety-related issues track back to underlying thinking problems.

Physical health can be hard to evaluate in terms of when to worry because many older adults live with chronic health problems. You're looking for issues that might be affecting daily life function or causing serious safety issues. In those cases, it may be time to be more proactive about involvement in a parent's healthcare. These are concerns that can impact quality of life or signal a health problem that warrants more care.

Mood and brain health are often overlooked dimensions of wellness. Again, here you're looking for issues that can affect everyday functioning and safety. Mood disorders and depression can be hard to distinguish from cognitive changes. One can lead to the other, and it's also possible to experience both at the same time.

Medication safety/management can be both a safety and physical health concern. Given the increased use of prescription and over-the-counter medication with age, the amounts of time and money they can consume, and possible side effects or problems associated with their misuse, this is an important category to separate out when considering the well-being of an older adult.

TOOL AND DOWNLOADABLE CHEATSHEET: LIFESKILLS & SAFETY PROBLEMS CHECKER

You can find a downloadable cheatsheet, "Life Skills & Safety Problems Checker," to use with this exercise by going to RESOURCES.

Check off which of these apply to your parent. Also, jot down some notes about your specific concerns relating to each. (There may naturally be some overlap with the Cognitive Symptom Checker, above—that's okay. Between the two tools, you're most likely to capture everything.)

Have you noticed any of the following?

Life Tasks

Any problems with the Activities of Daily Living?

- ☐ Walking and getting around (difficulty, especially on steps, tripping on feet, or dizzy when getting out of a chair)

- ☐ Dressing (choosing clothes appropriate to weather or event, wearing same clothes over and over, struggling to get clothes on)

- ☐ Trouble using the toilet independently or signs of accidents or incontinence

- ☐ Bathing (avoiding showers, smelling bad)

- ☐ Grooming (forgetting to shave, trouble fixing hair or applying makeup, looking unkempt)

- ☐ Feeding (not getting food into mouth, difficulty swallowing)

Any problems with Instrumental Activities of Daily Living?

- ☐ Finances (unopened or unpaid bills, trouble making change)

- ☐ Transportation (trouble driving, using public transit)

- ☐ Housecleaning and chores (unkempt home or yard)

- ☐ Shopping (lack of food or supplies in house, online buying sprees)

- ☐ Meal preparation (no longer cooking, dishes in sink)

- ☐ Using telephone and managing mail (unopened mail, stops answering calls)

- ☐ Managing medications (not taking as recommended, not refilling regularly)

Safety

Any safety concerns regarding finances?

- ☐ Problems paying bills (collection letters, unopened mail, electricity off)

- ☐ Signs of possible financial exploitation or scams (many sweepstakes notices, missing home objects, mysterious bills, expressed worries about money or requests for money)

- ☐ Sudden interest in risky investments (especially in schemes often marketed to older adults, like reverse mortgages or buying gold or coins)

Any safety concerns related to memory and thinking?

- ☐ Wandering or getting lost (on foot or driving)

- ☐ Problems forgetting about the stove or other home equipment

- ☐ Unsecured firearms or uncharacteristic carelessness with them

- ☐ Other concerns about poor safety awareness or poor judgment

Any safety concerns with driving?

- ☐ Accidents or close calls

- ☐ Dents or scrapes on car

- ☐ Unusual number of tickets

- ☐ Passengers feel worried (good test: would you let your parent drive you or a child?)

Any safety concerns suggesting elder abuse?

- ☐ Concern about emotional, verbal, or physical abuse (from family, paid helper, other)

- ☐ Concern someone is taking financial advantage

Any safety concerns about the living situation?

- ☐ Difficulty navigating stairs (or to reach bedroom, laundry)

- ☐ Dangerous amounts of clutter

- ☐ Inability to get in and out of the home

Physical Health

Have you noticed any of the following?

- ☐ Frequent ER visits or hospitalizations

- ☐ Obvious declines in strength or health

- ☐ Recent falls

- ☐ Weight loss or poor appetite

- ☐ Complaints of pain

- ☐ Complaints of other uncomfortable symptoms

- ☐ Decreased involvement in life activities due to health problems

- ☐ Anything that worries you or your parents when it comes to health

Mood/Brain Health

Have you noticed any of the following?

- ☐ Frequent sadness
- ☐ Loss of interest in activities your parent used to enjoy
- ☐ Marked changes in personality (more irritable, critical, depressed, anxious)
- ☐ Paranoia, delusions, or odd new beliefs
- ☐ Hopelessness
- ☐ Excessive or unusual worrying
- ☐ Memory problems
- ☐ Difficulty learning new things
- ☐ Difficulty getting organized
- ☐ Mistakes in driving
- ☐ Mistakes with finances
- ☐ Unusual spending of money
- ☐ Lack of social or purposeful activities
- ☐ Loneliness

Medication Safety/Management

Have you noticed any of the following?

- ☐ Difficulty affording prescriptions
- ☐ Not taking all prescriptions as recommended
- ☐ Not refilling medications regularly
- ☐ Skipping certain medications

☐ Side effects or worrisome symptoms related to medications

☐ Buying lots of supplements without consulting a physician, especially "memory boosting" kinds

Step 3: Talk to Other Family Members or "Informants"

Other people who play key roles in your parent's life may have useful perspectives that you don't see. These "interested others" may, like you, share a stake in his or her well-being. Their insights can either underscore what you're seeing or freshly inform what you can do.

Stakeholders might include:

- Your parent's partner. One partner may be covering for the other and therefore unwilling or unable to discuss much. (Sometimes both are propping up each other.) Or the partner may be relieved by an opening to share concerns.

- Your adult siblings, half-siblings, and/or step-siblings. Remember, each child has a unique relationship to a parent, with a unique perspective.

- Other relatives with a close relationship to you or your parent, especially those in close contact.

- Your parent's neighbors, especially longtime neighbors.

- Your parent's friends (or family friends). You may know members of their social circle you can reach out to, such as a member of a club, fraternal order, or a longtime hair stylist.

- Your parent's colleagues you know, if still working, for example coworkers in a small business or someone they routinely volunteer with.

- Members of a religious community, such as a church leader or someone in a smaller faith group.

There's a fine line between seeming nosy and the well-intentioned gathering of insights. *It's really important to approach this step from a curiosity/learning perspective.* Your goal here is simply to find out if anyone else has noticed anything concerning. It's NOT to try to convince them of your suspicions or to get them on board with a plan you have in mind.

As you ask around, it's important to also respect your parent's autonomy and privacy. Bear these guidelines in mind:

- **Express your motivation in a general way.** Let the person you're talking to know you're thinking about your parent and how things are going. Avoid seeming on the attack or being so pointed in your questions that the person feels put on the spot or like they'd be disloyal for saying what they think.

  Avoid phrasings like: "Don't tell my mother I'm asking you about her" (unless you have a relationship with the person that supports it). Or "I need to know if you think my dad needs to move into a nursing home."

  Instead, you could try: "I can't believe Mom's 70! What's your take on how she's doing?" "My dad always insists he's fine, but I can't help but worry when I'm away so much; do you think that's wrong?"

- **Try not to "lead the witness."** Ask open-ended questions that invite feedback rather than unloading about everything you're seeing and asking for corroboration.

  Avoid phrasings like: "Pop's memory is shot! Do you agree?"

  Instead you could try: "How does Pop's memory strike you these days?"

- **Be open-minded and neutral**. You might not like what you hear or you might not hear anything you find useful. Stay open to any possibility.

  Avoid responses like: "I think you're wrong" or "Can't you see this is a problem?!" Avoid criticizing the person's take.

Instead you could try: "Hmm, thanks for letting me know." "Well that's helpful to hear."

- **Ask from a place of concern and respect.** Imagine how your parent would feel to hear what you're asking. Back off if the person you're talking to doesn't seem receptive.

  Avoid phrasings like: "Mama's losing it and driving us crazy. Can you help me force her to sell her house?"

  Instead you could try: "My sister and I are kind of worried about Mama and how she's doing lately. How do you think she's been doing? Do you think we should be concerned?"

Here are some additional ways you could probe without prying:

- **Use a recent change as an opener:** "*Do you notice anything different about* Mom since her surgery, Dad?"

- **Make it about you:** "Hi, Mrs. Smith, it's Anna's daughter, Jane. *I'm always worried about her living alone* and when I ask, she insists she's fine. Do you think she's doing okay, or is there more I could do to help?" (Or "…do you think she's lonely/managing the same as usual/acting any different since Dad died?")

- **Invite a general update:** "Hey, Sis, *after your visit next week, let me know* how you think Mom and Dad are doing."

- **Appeal to familiarity:** "I haven't seen my father in a few weeks, *but you see him every day.* How do you think he's getting along?"

- **Ask about a parallel situation:** "*I heard that* Mrs. Smith moved to an assisted living community because of her memory. Do you ever see my dad *doing something like that?*"

- **Ask hypotheticals that might spur more talk:** "*What would you and Mom do if* you decided the house was too big to keep up with?"

- **Riff off the news.** "*I just heard a story about* how common memory trouble is over 80; do you think we'll ever have to worry about my father?"

Step 4: Double-Check to See If Any "Red Flag" Safety Issues Are Present

Among all the things covered so far, some changes really stand out, signaling a need to act with extra urgency and care. They say, "Don't walk. Run!"

These critical red flags are worth making an extra effort to look for:

- **Repeated car accidents** (whether or not anyone was injured). Driving red flags include multiple tickets for driving infractions or other vehicle damage/dents in a short period.

- **Repeated ER visits or hospitalizations.** It's especially worrisome if you don't know the cause. But even if you do, repeated hospital admits usually correspond to increased frailty and a need for assistance.

- **Actual financial losses.** A parent may disguise this information, but take note if you become aware of a large "swindle" or "bad deal" or other uncharacteristic setback involving large amounts, including giving away a big sum to an unlikely recipient. There may also be large bills due for items your parent clearly doesn't need or can't afford. Impaired judgment is one of the earliest signs of cognitive impairment and the person may need protection from additional financial losses.

- **Incidents involving the stove.** Anyone can leave a burner on once or twice. But signs of a fire suggest a more serious concern that puts your parent or others at risk.

- **Incidents involving firearms.** Almost half of people over 65 own guns, according to Pew Research Center. An accidental discharge or threats made with a gun should tip you over from watchful concern to actively stepping in.

- **Other signs of actual (as opposed to risk of) elder abuse.** Abuse can be physical, emotional, financial, or sexual. Examples may include unexplained injuries (bruises, welts, scars, broken bones), not being allowed to see the person (by a professional or other family caregiver), overhearing threatening or controlling behavior, missing belongings or cash, or repeated overbillings or overcharges.

In any of these cases, the situation has already moved into a higher-risk situation where it's often more ethically permissible to intervene, even if the older person objects, because there are clearer signs that they are a threat to themselves or others.

You still will be better off if you finish going through this book to understand the basic process for helping—especially the next chapter about having a thoughtful conversation with your parent before acting.

But where it's often reasonable to spend some time working out how you can help your parent, if you've noticed the safety issues above, you'll have to accelerate the process. That includes potentially notifying authorities such as Adult Protective Services (APS), the Department of Motor Vehicles (DMV), or sometimes law enforcement. (More on those options later in this book.)

Then, Review Where Things Stand

Now you have a rounder sense of the current situation.

It's possible that you may conclude what you're seeing isn't that worrisome. In a minority of cases, once you examine your concerns on a specific level, you get the sense that they're more about things you should keep an eye on, rather than should do something about right away.

It's really common to engage in disaster projecting—you see something upsetting and your worry leads you to jump to the worst possible outcome. (Mom lost her keys again and you're sure she has dementia and shouldn't live alone anymore—when the reality is more like, Mom lost her keys again and this might just be normal aging, otherwise she's okay, but you hate the fact that she's frail and insists on living alone at 89.)

In such cases, you're usually right to be concerned. And in a way, you're fortunate to be ahead of the curve. You can continue to monitor the situation for signs that your parent truly needs more help because it's likely this will eventually be the case. Best of all, you can use this "watchful waiting" time as an opportunity to foster or deepen your connection with your aging parent and gently help them prepare for what might be coming up as they get older. (Even if this is the case for you, keep reading; we cover these things in the next chapters in ways you might find relevant now.)

What's more likely, however, because it's more common, is that you've confirmed the presence of some worrisome signs. You feel justified about sensing that it's time to take some action. And you may have realized that there's more to consider than you thought.

So let's talk about what you can do next.

What This Looks Like: The Smiths and The Johnsons

Example 1: The Smiths

Zeke Smith (whom you met in the Introduction and is concerned about his father, who lives far away) starts by doing the following:

1. **Checking for worrisome signs that could indicate real memory or thinking problems:** Zeke notes the driving troubles and unpaid bills. His dad's checkbook included some unusual large payments to his next-door neighbors, Zeke noticed on a recent visit, although he didn't ask about them at the time.

2. **Checking for signs of problems with life tasks or safety:**

Albert is able to dress, groom, and feed himself okay (ADLs), although he takes more meals at the local diner than at home. As for his IADLs (those more complex life skills), it's unclear how well he's keeping up with money management. There were those collection notices and his checks to the neighbors are concerning too. Driving seems to be the biggest safety issue. In addition to the accidents, Zeke made a point of observing him as a passenger and saw him go right through a stop sign without noticing. His dad seems to be in generally good health, Zeke thinks, other than becoming more wobbly and less organized.

3. **Talking to other family members and "informants:"** Zeke's siblings agree, when he finally brings it up with them, about the concerning changes; his sister mentions that Albert seems to wear the same clothes over and over and forgot several doctor appointments the last time she visited. When Zeke reaches out to his dad's longtime next-door neighbors, old friends, they seem relieved; they ask if he knows that Albert has gotten lost twice while driving to town and mention he keeps writing huge checks to them (which they don't cash) for doing small favors like mowing his lawn.

4. **Double-checking to see if any "red flag" issues are present:** Considering the frequency of accidents, what Zeke and his sister have observed, and getting lost, the driving issues seem to be a bigger safety issue than Zeke first thought. His sister has pointed out that she avoids having her kids be driven by their grandfather during visits because she doesn't think he's careful enough. The writing of large checks suggests that Albert is at high risk of financial exploitation too.

Zeke concludes that it's getting unsafe for his father to drive but isn't sure how to get him to give up the keys or if that's even practical. How would he get around? And then there's the question of how well he's managing finances: Zeke worries his father is incurring late fees and could even have services cut off. And he's at risk for writing inappropriate checks, maybe even vulnerable to scammers. His sister agrees with all this but their other sibling wants to wait and see—"Maybe it's not so bad."

They wonder if Albert should move closer to one of them or how else to keep him safe.

Example 2: The Johnsons

Sue Johnson (whom you also met in the Introduction) is worried about the many changes she's noticed in her mother since her father's death. She starts by doing the following:

1. **Checking for worrisome signs that could indicate real memory or thinking problems:** Going through the list of eight signs makes Sue realize that many of them apply. Her mom, who once walked and visited friends often with her late husband, now spends much of the day in an easy chair, staring out the window. Maria often seems sad and her mood is down. That said, she always perks up when her grandson is around. She dislikes driving lately and sometimes asks Sue to take her to the store; once Sue noticed she tried to pay for groceries with her insurance card, thinking it was a credit card. She's gotten very forgetful and often seems confused about the day of the week.

2. **Checking for signs of problems with life tasks or safety:** Maria is managing her own grooming, dressing, and bathing; she no longer does much laundry, cleaning, or food prep. Once an enthusiastic cook, Maria seems to have trouble following through in the kitchen. Her daughter often finds half-started projects there, along with spoiled food in the fridge. Recently, she arrived to find a charred pot burning on the stove. Maria has always been quite overweight but hasn't let this slow her down until recently.

3. **Talking to other family members and "informants:"** Sue's Aunt Jane, Maria's sister, pooh-poohs any suggestion of trou-

ble and blames sadness. When Sue asks her mom's longtime hairdresser and friend how she thinks her mom is doing, the woman mentions that Maria forgot her last two appointments and has an outstanding bill because she forgot her purse another time. She's noticed memory problems for quite a while and says she thinks Maria's late husband was covering for her lapses and handling many day-to-day details.

4. **Double-checking to see if any "red flag" issues are present:** Sue still thinks that the burning pot was a one-time mistake but feels she needs to watch things more closely.

The assessment leaves Sue feeling that she's right to be uneasy about changes in her mother's thinking skills and mood, despite people like her aunt telling her that this is just part of the grieving process. She worries about her being alone all day—but isn't really sure how serious things are or what she should do next.

Chapter 2:
Next, Get Your Parent's Take

As essential as it is to identify potential health problems and life needs, it's not enough. The very next thing to do after sizing up an aging parent's concerning situation is…to talk to your parent.

Don't skip this step! Even if you've already tried talking to them—and if you're like many of the families who write to Dr. K, you have—chances are good that you haven't yet been talking in quite the right way. Which is *to "talk" with the intention of listening.*

This is the way a geriatrician approaches a patient, especially one who is reluctant or resistant.

What this isn't: A talk in which you tell your parent what you think needs to be done. It's not about convincing, persuading, hinting, encouraging, cajoling, or even problem-solving. Not yet.

Instead, you simply want to listen intently, to learn more about what they're thinking, feeling, and preferring.

Why This Conversation Matters

Aging care experts know it's important to start with a preliminary conversation with the patient (your parent/s) that covers getting their perspective of where things stand and a sense of their concerns and priorities. What you learn may confirm your suspicions and the information you've gathered so far. Or, and maybe you should expect this, what you hear may be very different. It's all useful.

Having such a talk is worthwhile even if your parent seems uncooperative, annoyed, or angry. You might hear things that sound crazy, paranoid, irrational, or unrealistic. If that's how they see it, you and your family need to know. It's actually very useful to know if an older person's assessment is wildly at odds with that others are observing or concluding.

Plus, this initial, open-ended talk with your parent will serve several additional important purposes:

- **It can help soften any resistance.** Anyone is more likely to listen or accept help when he or she feels heard. We're all wired this way. Logical arguments often fail to convince us where emotional relationships or issues are involved. This is true at any age or any state of mental sharpness. Especially if an issue stirs up feelings connected to our self-worth, identity, or autonomy—as is so often the case here—emotions become powerful drivers of our reactions. So before you can direct, you need to connect.

  Emotional validation—feeling heard, understood, and valued—opens receptiveness. It also reduces stress, which is all the more important if there's potential dementia because reducing stress and building security help the brain function better.

- **It can move you toward more workable fixes.** It's not enough to get your take and your siblings' take. The better you understand how your parent sees things, and the clearer an understanding you gain of his or her goals and priorities, the better you can tailor your suggestions to fit in with their desires. Finding solutions that address your parent's underlying needs will improve the odds of success. *It's a classic geriatrician tactic to frame all of our helpful suggestions as ways to help an older person attain or keep something that's important to them.*

It's important to recognize that your parent's goals might not be the same as yours. (More about this key insight in a moment.)

- **It can build relationship capital.** A conversation based on respectful listening helps bring you closer, whether you're already tight or sometimes at odds. Reinforcing your relationship is important because you're going to need to draw on as much goodwill as you can in the weeks ahead.

- **It can help you understand what's been done medically so far.** Not least, your exchange may give you a sense of what, if anything, your parent has discussed with a doctor. That's useful to know as you determine next steps.

Remember to keep your focus on relationship building and information gathering.

TOOL: WHAT TO SAY/WHAT NOT TO SAY WHEN APPROACHING A PARENT ABOUT CONCERNS

Exactly what you say will depend on the situation, your relationship, and whether you've ever talked about the situation or your concerns before. What's key, whatever the circumstances: start in a natural, conversational way, and open with broad or general questions, rather than launching into a specific complaint or concern.

You might even start with something very generic, like "How are you feeling?" or "How's the house?" as a way to test the waters on their mood or openness to talking more, just then.

Here are more sample approaches:

"I've noticed that you sometimes [insert an observation, like: have trouble taking all these pills]. Can we talk about it? I was wondering if you had noticed any changes in how you're doing and what you thought of them."

"I see that [insert an observation, like you almost fell on those old steps]. Is that happening a lot?"

"Tell me the best and worst things about [insert an expressed or observed problem, like: keeping up with all these bills]. Maybe we can figure out how to make it better."

"You seem [insert an emotional state, like: frustrated/sad/worried/preoccupied]...so I've been a little worried. What are your thoughts about [insert a possible issue, like: how you keep forgetting where you parked the car?" (Or "What did your doctor have to say about that?")

"Can I help you with that?" (in response to a topic that's been complained about, like: a new medication).

"I've been thinking about where I'll live when I retire and was wondering what you think about [insert a concern you're seeing in your parent that you can personalize, like: whether it's a good idea our two-story house or not]."

"You know I really care about you—I'd like to make sure I understand more about what you've been feeling about [insert observation about an issue, like: not being able to drive at night anymore]."

"You know I want what's best for you and makes you happiest. That's why I'm curious what would you like to see happen if [insert a hypothetical, like: you couldn't climb the stairs to this house or your room anymore]."

"How are you feeling about [insert a parallel situation from the news or a friend, like: Mrs. Smith moving away]? Would you ever want to do that?"

Useful follow-up phrases

These can keep the conversation going:

"Hmm, tell me more." (Both neutral and encouraging, this is one of the most useful responses you can offer—especially if they've just said something that sounds a bit nutty.)

"Can you say more about that?"

"What's the most important part of that for you?"

"What else is on your mind?"

"Would you like me to help you get some more information about that?"

"What if things got worse; what would you like to see happen?"

"Anything else?"

What NOT to say:

Avoid saying things that could be interpreted as telling them how they should or shouldn't feel, or what they should or shouldn't do:

"Why don't you…"

"You need to…"

"What you really should do is…"

"What's taking so long?"

"I don't understand why you haven't…"

"We need to make a decision about…"

"The doctor said you should…"

"That's exactly why you should…"

"Like I keep telling you…"

"You obviously should…"

"When are you going to…?"

"Here's what I'm going to do."

DOWNLOADABLE CHEATSHEET: HOW TO SAY IT: COMMUNICATING BETTER WITH YOUR PARENT WHEN YOU HAVE CONCERNS

For a quick guide, you might want to print this companion resource.

As You Listen: Stay Clear About Your Goals vs. Your Parent's

As you listen to your parent's take on things, be aware that what's driving him or her in this situation may not be the same thing that's driving you. Especially when there's conflict or resistance, realizing differences in your goals and motivations can help untangle sticky situations.

Common underlying issues for adult children:

- Minimizing guilt. You want to feel like you're doing your part.

- Fear. Of your parent getting hurt or sick, or dying, or that they'll decline further and require more help.

- Wariness around conflict with other siblings. Disagreements may be the legitimate discord of two divergent ways to view a situation or deeply embedded resentments and disagreements-for-disagreement's-sake.

- Wanting a parent to be happy and comfortable.

- Needing to know what will happen next or to resolve an issue quickly in order to return to the rest of your life.

- Discomfort over role reversals, help tasks, or seeing your parent as weak.

- Projecting how you'd like your own old age to look.

- Wanting your parent to do the things that are good for their health.

Compare these with the common underlying motivations of older parents:

- Living in their own home as long as possible.

- Independence.

- Maintaining a sense of control (dictating the terms of their daily life, making major choices).

- Living their usual life for as long as possible (such as driving, cooking, social activities).

- Minimizing pain, illness, and suffering (sometimes while not being too bothered about doing everything the doctors recommend).

- Spending quality time with family and loved ones.

- A good quality of life (more enjoyable activities and fewer stressful or burdensome activities).

Safety is a huge, common point of conflict. Don't fall into the trap of assuming it should be your family's top concern. Adult children (and doctors!) tend to prioritize staying safe, along with longevity. We want to prevent accidents, falls, injuries, illnesses, new medical problems, and dangers of any kind. We'd like our parents to live forever, or at least as long as possible. It might even seem wrong not to want a person to live as long as they can.

Most older adults, when faced with a trade-off between safety and independence, however, choose independence. Even when cognitive problems like dementia are present, a certain amount of risk is usually considered a worthwhile trade-off if it preserves some self-control and quality of life.

Tips for a Better Initial Talk With Your Parent

To help it go well:

Know that it's likely to take more than one conversation. As awkward and painful as these talks can be for some, it's rare that you get a full understanding of your parent's perspective in one swoop. It's often easier on both sides to revisit the topic several times.

Aim for a 1:1. Even if you're collaborating with another sibling or your partner, you might have more success talking solo with your parent. See if you can agree on a spokesperson ahead of time. Some parents are receptive to having such conversations in a group but for others it can feel like "ganging up." If your parent starts out on the defensive, it's less likely to be a constructive conversation.

Pick the right setting and time. Make sure you're not competing with the TV, radio, or a roomful of relatives. Being outside or enjoying a treat together can help you both relax. Choose a time when your parent is most likely to feel rested and alert; many older adults have more energy and focus in the morning. But if you know your parent isn't a morning person, pick a better time. And while a holiday visit might seem convenient, it can put a damper on a happy time so your parent might not be responsive.

Give it time. Many older adults take a while to dive into a deeper conversation, especially if they're having trouble with vision, hearing, or mobility. In fact, normal cognitive aging by itself means that older adults need more time to weigh complex issues, especially those that trigger negative emotions. Avoid diving in with, "Mom, we need to talk about your living situation!" You might ease in with small talk about the weather or your dog first. As you ask questions, allow plenty of space for answers; don't be in a rush to fill pauses or silences yourself with chatter.

Assume nothing. This isn't about who's right and who's wrong. It's about exploring what your parent feels and values, how he or she sees things. Best to go into this conversation expecting you won't see things exactly the same way because most parents and adult children don't. Conflicts and trade-offs are likely. Or what you hear may not be logical or wise.

Ask questions instead of making statements. Let this be your rule of thumb during your conversation, no matter what you're tempted to say. Listening is more important than telling.

Watch blame-loaded words. Stick to "I" statements ("I'm wondering/I'm curious/I've noticed") over "you" comments ("You always/you keep/your problem is…"). Try to stay away from generalizations like *always, never, everything, nothing.*

Don't get undermined by your own body language. Believe it or not, studies show that more of a message gets communicated through nonverbal ways than through words, and what you're *not* saying can undermine you. Examples of cues to avoid: frowning, sighing, tense shoulders, lack of eye contact, standing over someone seated, pointing fingers, crossing your arms in front of you (which signals confrontation and not being open).

Be a good listener. You can reinforce the sense of being heard and re-spected by mirroring back or paraphrasing what your parent is saying: "So you wish you could stay in this house forever." "You sound worried about your memory." Or even, "I'm hearing you say that you don't think anything is wrong with you." "So you don't want to talk about this right now?" Avoid interrupting.

Put your own feelings aside. Try not to react with frustration or ex-asperation. Above all, try not to take resistance or rejection personally. Remember, the emotional brain is ruling in these kinds of talks so you might have to make extra effort to stay neutral.

Don't try to solve anything yet. You might feel like once you've dived into a subject with your parent that you need to take it to the conclu-sion—a solution. Instead, avoid getting caught up in moving toward, or even talking about, how to fix things at this point. It's better to build rapport and collect information.

TOOL: WHAT TO SAY TO KEEP THINGS NEUTRAL

You can put off getting drawn into premature problem-solving (or ar-guing, if your parent's views seem unrealistic) by using phrases that reassure or move the conversation forward in a neutral way, like:

- "Okay, so that's really important to you. *That's good to know as we figure out a way forward.*"

- "*Why don't I look into this* before we decide anything."

- "We can research some options; *let's talk again after* we have more information."

- "I hear you saying X. *In case that doesn't pan out, it's also worth thinking about Y.*"

- "Now that I understand what's important to you, *let's both think a little more and talk again.*"

- "Sure, *let's both give some time to considering the pros and cons on each possibility.*"

- "*It really helps to hear what you're thinking.* Let's talk more later."

How to Tell If You Should Drop It (For Now)

It's best not to press a conversation that's not going anywhere. If your parent is really resistant to talking about it, don't force the issue.

Signs you should stop for now:

- Your parent is growing visibly angry.

- Your parent starts to cry.

- Your parent keeps turning the conversation to irrelevant topics.

- You begin to argue.

- You're having a hard time controlling your temper.

- Your parent refuses to engage at all.

- Your parent leaves the room. (Don't follow and keep talking!)

Better to abort this attempt for now and bring it up again, maybe in a different way, another day.

If You've Already Approached Your Parent and It's Gone Badly, Try Again

What if you've tried before to talk to your parent and gotten nowhere?

That would make you very typical!

People being people, we all have a tendency to try to address our needs (less guilt, less fear, whatever) by wanting *others* to do something differently that aligns better with our views or by trying to keep things from changing. Trouble is, meeting our needs by controlling others is seldom very effective.

If you've tried to push your agenda or solution too fast, too far, or without laying any groundwork, it's apt to be met with resistance.

Chances are that in previous conversations, your parent felt that you were trying to undermine his or her independence or take away control. Or they may have felt you pooh-poohed their concerns or priorities. When we feel misunderstood, or worse yet, threatened, resistance is inevitable. It often wins out over logic (for example, you're accused of "butting in where you have no business" even when your parent obviously needs help).

Remember emotions are running high—your parent's as well as your own. He or she may also be feeling vulnerable or frightened by what's going on at the moment. A recent change (a diagnosis, a partner's death, an injury) can feel overwhelming. Some people feel guilty or even angry about the prospect of being seen as weak or becoming a burden.

Furthermore, even if you brought ninja communication skills to the first encounter, many older adults need to be approached more than once and they need some time to reflect and digest between conversations. All of this explains why trying to help an older parent often goes off the rails on the first try.

But that doesn't have to be the end of the story. Offering support is an ongoing opportunity.

TOOL: WHAT TO SAY, TAKE 2

To try again:

1. Be especially mindful about choosing a good time and place.

2. Pick a different kind of opener than the one that didn't go so well last time.

3. Whether you refer to your earlier conversation can depend on how it went.

Sample reopeners:

"I keep thinking about those collection agency calls. What are you thinking you might do about that?"

"You know how I was asking you how you feel about driving? What would you like to see happen?"

"I'm still worried about your forgetting to refill your prescriptions. Can I help?"

To hit reset when things went off the rails, you want to:

1. Apologize for past efforts.

2. Explain that you're coming from a place of concern and help, not judgment or bossiness, and you really want to understand how your parent sees things.

3. Validate, validate, validate what you hear them saying or expressing, without judging it or leaving them feeling they are "wrong."

4. Ask them to help you understand.

Sample apologies:

"I guess I spoke too fast before; I'm sorry if I came across like I don't care

what you think. Let's take a giant step backward on all this. I just want to understand your feelings and priorities better. What would you like to see happen?"

"I apologize if it sounded like I was telling you what to do. Obviously, it's your life and you're in charge of it. I was just so worried. Help me understand what you're thinking about this situation so I can help you better."

"I'm sorry I lost my temper when we talked before. The last thing I want to do is upset you. Let's try again and this time, how about I just listen? Tell me what's important to you and I promise to try to help you make that happen, if we can."

"If you felt hurt when I brought up X, I'm very sorry. That was just my clumsy way of wanting to help. I've realized I skipped over how YOU feel about all this. So now I'd really like to hear that."

With luck and care, you can open the gates to honest conversations about what's going on. As difficult as these talks can be, and even if your parent's responses seem completely off-base, they can shape what happens next. Now it's also possible that despite your most gentle, respectful, and persistent efforts, your parent may still stonewall you. In some cases, a cognitive or mental health issue may be interfering with the ability to have any degree of clarity about a situation. In other cases, family history can get in the way of collaborative talk. And it's just hard!

At least you've tried. However your attempts to get your older parent's take on things has gone, at least your talk should have given you some insights on how they see the situation, how they feel about your concern, and what seems to be important to them.

Between these insights and the information you gathered in Chapter 1, you're now in a great position to research some options and plan the next steps.

What This Looks Like:
The Smiths and The Johnsons

Example 1: The Smiths

Zeke Smith, who lives a state away from his father, Albert, has determined that while his dad seems to be managing daily care all right, despite taking a few recent falls around the house, he should probably stop driving (a safety red flag). He's had three minor accidents and gotten lost twice in the past six months. Zeke's two siblings, whom he's consulted, agree there have been changes but are busy with their own lives and don't seem willing to intervene.

Zeke is also concerned that Albert is having trouble keeping up with paperwork and finances.

Zeke calls his dad to get his take.

Son: "You know, I keep thinking about those car accidents and that ticket you got. It's been quite a couple of years—does it worry you?"

Father: "What ticket? I didn't get a ticket. And those fender benders were the other driver's fault."

Son: "Well, I saw the ticket when I was at your house. It was overdue and if I remember right, you had to pay an extra fine."

Father: "No, that wasn't me. Anyway, my driving is fine."

Son: "Ok, well, maybe I misunderstood regarding the ticket. Well, I guess it's just that, along with those tumbles you took in the house, I worry if you're having some kind of physical issue that's making it harder. Sissy just asked me the same thing the other day. So we're just wondering how you felt about it."

Father: "Oh, I'm fine. What falls? And what does that have to do with my driving? I drive every day, just fine."

It's clear to Zeke that his father won't easily consent to giving up his keys. Not only does he not even acknowledge that there's a problem with his driving ability, he doesn't seem to remember some of the incidents. Zeke brings up the financial and memory concerns next.

Son: "Well, Dad, it's not just us worrying. The neighbors mentioned that you'd gotten lost in the car and that you were writing them some big checks."

Father: "The neighbors are just mad at me."

Son: "Oh? Tell me more about that."

Father: "Well, they won't let me pay them for mowing the lawn!"

Son: "Well, $500 is an awfully big amount. That's how much they said you wrote a check for."

Father: "Oh, well, my checkbook is my business. And so is my car! You should all stay out of it!"

Son: "I know it's hard to keep up with all the paperwork, plus everything else that comes in the mail these days. I just wondered if I might be able to help; you know I have time."

Father: "I'm fine."

Son: "What does old Doc Lee say? I know you had to see him a lot after you fell."

Father: "Fit as a fiddle!"

Son: "That's great. When did you last see him?"

Father: "Oh, I don't know. I think I'm fine."

Son: "Well, what's he recommending you do to take care of yourself these days?"

Father: "He says I should just keep taking my pills."

Son: "No worries about your memory, though?"

Father: "Smart as a whip!"

The longer they talk, the more Zeke realizes that his father doesn't see any problems or want any help. He's just the way he's always been, proud and independent. But also either unaware or in significant denial of what's going on. None of this is a surprise but useful for Zeke and his siblings to know as they figure out what to do next.

Example 2: The Johnsons

Sue Johnson is realizing that her mother, Maria, who lives alone near-by, is having a great deal of trouble with her home and financial management. She's also pretty sure that her mom hasn't seen a doctor about the memory concerns.

Daughter: "Mom, it scared me when I found that burning pot on the stove the other day. I feel like there have been a lot of mistakes like that lately that you didn't used to make. What do you think?"

Mother: "Well, we all make mistakes. I'm just getting older. It's hard since your father died."

Daughter: "Yes, I know you miss Dad. I do too. But it's been almost a year and you don't get out like you used to. You don't even cook or get your hair done anymore. How are you really feeling? Maybe you could see a doctor to get checked?"

Mother [angry]: "Well if you think I'm losing my mind like May Jones, I'm not!"

Daughter: "Can you tell me more about what you mean?"

Mother: "You think I have that Alzheimer's too!"

Daughter: "I didn't say that. I just hate to see you not seeming yourself and asked how you're feeling, if maybe a doctor could help."

Mother: "You know I hate doctors."

Daughter [shifting the focus as she senses her mother is becoming upset]: "Well, how do you feel about managing all the bills? How else can I help you?"

Mother: "Oh, you do so much. It's nice of you to bring me dinner every day. Maybe sometimes we can talk about your helping with the money stuff."

Sue senses that her mother knows she's slipping a little but is fearful because she watched her best friend, May, go through early-onset Alzheimer's. She seems willing to accept a little help but not much. And Sue works full time and can't micromanage everything. She wonders if a doctor could help but her mother hasn't had a regular doctor in years. She knows her mom would be very resistant to getting checked, especially about memory concerns. Still, she feels like bringing up these concerns is opening the door a crack.

Daughter: "It sounds like you've had a lot going on since Dad died. It really helps me to hear how you're thinking. Yeah, let's talk about it some more later."

Mother: "You're so good to me."

Although Sue still isn't sure what to do next, she now has a better sense of how her mom views things (Alzheimer's worry—yes, see a doctor—no, open to more help—yes). And that makes her feel a tiny bit more optimistic.

PART TWO: TAKING AIM

A ROADMAP OF WHAT SHOULD HAPPEN NEXT (EVEN IF IT RARELY WORKS OUT THIS WAY)

Hopefully, you now have a pretty good sense of the situation, at least from your vantage point and your parent's (Part One). Now you're ready to figure out what to do next to address the issues you've identified.

This section (Part Two) maps out the *ideal* progression of next steps that geriatricians and other experts would recommend. "Ideal" is the key word here; most people won't be able to make everything we outline happen, in the described way, on the first try.

That's less a reflection on you than the situation and on the realities of helping an aging person through a difficult time. Because here's the thing: Helping an older parent is almost always challenging, no matter what your ability, personality, skill set, or how much you care. Just how hard will also depend on your parent, the rest of your family, the medical landscape you encounter, and other considerations.

Some of you will find yourselves in a situation where you can quickly make a difference. For the majority of readers, however, the path to helping is apt to be slower, more stop-and-go (and sometimes 'round-in-circles). We'll show you why this is so.

Chapter 3 first outlines the *optimal* approach for most situations, almost always beginning with a medical evaluation (we go into lots of specifics about why, how to prepare, and what to hope for). It goes hand-in-hand with Chapter 4, which you'll want to follow-up with quickly for reassurance that yes, if you have trouble implementing the ideal steps of Chapter 3, you're far from alone and here's why.

Once you go through these two chapters, however, you'll be much better equipped to chart your path forward, anticipating the bumps and complications that usually come up. Think of it as a sketch of the bigger picture of eldercare that you're working within; knowing this context will save you time and headaches in the long run and increase your odds of a better experience.

Chapter 3:
Learn the Ideal Approach to Aim For

Let's look at the steps that, in a perfect world where you could control everything, can most quickly and effectively make a difference. Aim as best you can toward those that apply to your situation to spare you time and trouble down the road.

(Ideally...) Get a Medical Evaluation

Many of you will be wondering if this is "dementia" or "Alzheimer's" or *what*. Whether you're certain you're dealing with a failing memory (based on your experiences in Chapter 1) or aren't sure what's going on, you'll want to push for a medical evaluation.

Most of the time, problems and declines affecting an older adult can be traced back to an underlying medical problem.

That's why your family needs to try to find out what underlying medical issue is causing the problems you're observing in your parent. The results of the medical evaluation will influence how you go forward and may even change the direction of how to best improve the current situation.

HOW A CHECKUP HELPS YOUR PARENT AND YOU

- **An evaluation can independently document the presence (or absence) of cognitive impairment** (a broad term for some kind of problem in memory or thinking skills or other mental processes, beyond normal "cognitive aging").

  Why this is important: Having a clearer picture of cognitive status can guide your decision-making and how assertively you may need to step in. A good initial evaluation should include an objective office-based assessment of your parent's thinking and should also start the ball rolling on looking into the *cause* of the thinking problems.

  Some causes of cognitive trouble are treatable or even reversible. Or if dementia is confirmed, this also allows you to begin the necessary future care planning. Knowing for sure can also make it easier to deal with personality changes and difficult behaviors with more compassion.

  Note: Because a single visit provides only a snapshot of functioning at that time, it may take more than one visit to verify what's going on.

- **An evaluation can identify any other health problems that may be affecting the mind's function.** Undiagnosed or improperly treated conditions (both chronic and acute) may be causing or worsening cognitive symptoms or other impairments.

  Why this is important: Properly treating these conditions can lessen or even reverse symptoms. Even in people who clearly have dementia, brain function can be improved when certain issues are addressed.

- **An evaluation can help establish a baseline,** if you don't already have one, by which future concerns can be measured.

  Why this is important: Depending on the cause, cognitive impairment can sometimes be temporary and may or may not slowly continue to worsen. Having a clinically documented assessment becomes a measuring stick for gauging change that's useful for providers to have as they try to figure out what's going on.

- **An evaluation is an opportunity to get a medication review.** This is basically a recheck of every prescription and over-the-counter medication or supplement the person takes.

Why this is important: Some medications aren't "brain safe" and can cause worrisome symptoms or can make a weakening brain worse than it otherwise would be. There may be better alternatives. Also, many prescriptions are "forgotten" over time—initially prescribed but perhaps no longer useful, recommended, or safe. The more medication an older adult takes, the greater the risk of side effects and dangerous interactions. It also saves money if your parent can be taken off medications that have outlived their usefulness.

- **If your parent is having difficulty with thinking or with life tasks, your parent's doctors need to know.** Ideally, you work with your parent's medical team to address needs and make future plans.

Why this is important: Beyond the obvious reason that you want the doctor's help in investigating any cognitive impairment or other decline, this has repercussions for future health management. If your parent is impaired, they're going to be less able to manage the "self-healthcare" that the doctor usually expects a patient to handle, such as properly taking medications, monitoring for symptoms, and so on. That's why it's critical that your parent's doctors be aware if your parent is struggling so that they can consider simplifying (or otherwise altering) your parent's healthcare or involving family. Remember, families often detect cognitive changes first, even before the doctor does so don't sit back and wait for changes to hopefully be picked up at some future checkup.

- **An evaluation can shape how you go forward from here.** Ideally, you work with your parent's medical team to address needs and make future plans.

  Why this is important: understanding someone's cognitive status and any medical reasons behind concerns is an important grounding for everything that follows—from practical and ethical perspectives.

You want this to be a fast and efficient process. You don't want it to drag on for months with endless appointments and no conclusive help at the end of it. Above all, you don't want it done incorrectly.

Here's how to get what you need.

MAKING AN APPOINTMENT: OPTIONS

At this stage, many people are unclear about what's already been done, medically. Has your parent already expressed concerns to a doctor and had an earlier evaluation? Or has the doctor noticed anything?

You can try asking directly: "What does your doctor think? Have you had a checkup recently?" Or ask your parent's partner. If they say yes, you want to find out as much as you can about the results and what was said.

Unless the appointment was recent and you have a full report of the results, though, you'll want to help your parent schedule a medical visit specifically for evaluation of cognitive impairment.

You have several choices for where to get an initial evaluation:

A primary care physician. The simplest, most practical starting place for most people is your parent's primary care doctor. This physician is most likely a general practitioner or internist. Or your parent may already see, or you may want to try to consult, a geriatrician (a specialist in aging care).

Even within the real-world constraints of a short visit, it's possible to cover the necessary basics that will give the doctor a sense of what's going on and what kind of follow-up is needed. Whether this happens or not depends on the doctor you see, unfortunately.

A neurologist. A general neurologist will generally be able to evaluate cognitive impairment. Many primary providers will refer out to a neurologist in their network if concerns about cognitive impairment are brought up.

In Dr. K's experience, the quality of a neurologist's evaluation for this purpose is variable. These specialists tend to be good at ordering tests and ruling out other medical conditions. They may not, however, offer as much practical support in coping with safety and function problems as a specialized clinic or a dementia specialist.

A multidisciplinary memory clinic. This is the "Cadillac" option for getting a detailed evaluation and diagnosis. These clinics, often based at universities, have a lot of time and staff to do a comprehensive, in-depth evaluation. They may also have social workers available and sometimes can help families get enrolled in special support programs. On the other hand, the lengthy evaluation takes a lot of time and effort and it often takes months to get an appointment. It's not feasible in many locations. And it may not be necessary, given other available options. In general, special memory clinics are most likely to be helpful to those people who develop memory or thinking problems when they are younger (say, younger than 75) or when the initial evaluation leaves a primary care provider or neurologist feeling stumped.

Other specialists to consider. There are other medical experts who can sometimes be involved in a cognitive impairment evaluation. Two specialties to be aware of are:

- *Neuropsychologists.* Neuropsychologists are trained to do detailed office-based cognitive testing that is much more thorough than the shorter tests used by geriatricians, primary care providers, and neurologists. Neuropsychological testing can take up to three to five hours, although sometimes a shorter test is possible. Neuropsychological testing is often included as part of the extensive evaluation done by memory clinics or other specialized centers.

- ***Geriatric psychiatrists.*** Geriatric psychiatry is a subspecialty of psychiatry. These providers have particular training and experience in evaluating cognitive impairment in aging adults. They can be especially helpful when it comes to evaluating memory or thinking problems in older adults who have a history of serious mental illness. The downside is that they are even rarer than geriatricians so it can be hard to get an appointment.

Bottom line: Dr. K generally recommends starting with your parent's primary care provider if they have one. This doctor should be able to do an initial evaluation, especially if you give them a heads up and come prepared. Even if they're unwilling to do so and decide to refer out to a neurologist (which is common) or special memory clinic (less common but possible), it's important for your parent's regular doctor to know that you and your family are concerned about your parent's memory, thinking, and/or safety.

DOWNLOADABLE CHEATSHEET: TEN POSSIBLE CAUSES OF COGNITIVE IMPAIRMENT AND TEN THINGS DOCTORS SHOULD CHECK

These lists can help you understand what the doctor is looking for and what they should do to make a faster and better assessment of possible dementia. See RESOURCES.

Be forewarned that not every doctor may do all these things unless a family member is there to look for them, ask about them, and advocate for the patient. Here's a situation where it pays to be proactive.

Note: It can take more than one visit to evaluate cognitive impairment and make a diagnosis because the doctor may need to order tests, obtain past medical records, and gather other information. There's no single definitive "dementia test." Diagnosing Alzheimer's and other forms of dementia requires ruling out other medical conditions—it's a bit like

---

playing detective!

Don't rely on your parent's Medicare Annual Wellness Visit to provide the kind of cognitive assessment and evaluation that's needed. This benefit may be a way to get a really reluctant person to the doctor and it is supposed to include a cognitive screening. But studies show that many doctors skip that part and the assessment isn't done in any standard, detailed way.

BEFORE THE APPOINTMENT: DETERMINE HOW COMFORTABLE YOUR PARENT IS WITH YOUR BEING THERE

Ideally you—or another trusted person—should attend this appointment with your parent. Someone experiencing cognitive symptoms isn't the most reliable reporter of what's going on. If your parent attends alone, any findings might be lost in translation by the time he or she conveys them to you or forgotten entirely. Most important, the more information that family members and other "informants" can provide, the closer the doctor will be to putting together enough pieces for a diagnosis.

Your parent may be willing to get checked with you present if he or she...

- Has an awareness of changes and an active interest in getting to the bottom of it.

- Lacks awareness of change but is willing to listen to your concerns.

- Lacks awareness of change but is amenable to cooperating with you.

Your parent may be resistant to getting checked with you present, however, if he or she...

- Is unwilling to involve you in medical care (whether or not he/she has concerns).

• Is in denial about cognitive changes.

What's most important is that someone is present who's able to be proactive and take notes on what the provider says. Your parent may prefer to have a partner/spouse present instead of you. This is only problematic if you feel that person is also having cognitive issues or won't be candid with you, for whatever reasons (covering for the partner, the nature of their relationship with you). In that event, see Chapter 6 on common obstacles.

If your parent is resistant about your coming to the appointment, or resistant to getting checked at all, also see Chapter 6, where we cover possible solutions to try.

AT THE APPOINTMENT: WHAT TO BRING AND BE PREPARED TO SAY

Effectively evaluating a patient when there are cognitive concerns should be a deliberate process. It's not good enough for a doctor to simply note "confusion, unknown timing, probable dementia," which Dr. K often sees reported in physician notes. Families also tell of long-time doctors who dismiss symptoms with a reassuring, "Oh, we're all getting older."

The more information that can be assessed in the evaluation, the better.

Here's a summary of the most important things.

Try to Bring with You:

• The information you've collected about memory and other thinking skills, problems with everyday life skills or abilities, or recent changes in personality or behavior. If you've made written documentation of incidents and concerns, bring it.

• Copies of your parent's medical information, if there are records from other doctors. Copies of any labs or brain imaging reports (MRIs, CT scans) are especially useful.

- Medications, vitamins, supplements, and over-the-counter medications currently being taken. The actual containers are more helpful than a medication list. If you have it, also bring a list of medications that have been prescribed in the past but aren't currently being taken.

Be Prepared to Communicate:

- Your specific impressions of what's going on, including any particular safety issues.

- How symptoms, behaviors, or everyday abilities have been changing over time. Try to be specific about how your parent is managing life tasks such as driving, cooking, work responsibilities, or household chores.

- Any recent falls, illnesses, or hospitalizations your parent has had for which they saw a different doctor.

- Any history of mental illness, including depression or anxiety (or symptoms of these conditions) your parent has.

You may be worried that it will distress or upset your parent to hear you describe some of the above to the doctor. In our experience, many older adults with impairments feel angry or embarrassed when their adult child or someone else talks about all the things they've been doing "wrong."

So be sure to consider ahead of time the various ways you might communicate this essential info to your parent's health providers. If you think it will upset your parent to hear you say these things in front of them, it's often possible to convey the information more discreetly. For instance, you may be able to tell the doctor's medical assistant that you'd like to tell them a few things before (preferable) or after the visit. Dr. K also recommends summarizing your findings in a letter that you can bring to the appointment and give to the medical assistant before the exam. If you can do so without your parent's awareness, say that you'd also like to briefly talk to the doctor and have also provided a written recap for his or her convenience.

DOWNLOADABLE CHEATSHEET: WHAT TO BRING TO A COGNITIVE/DEMENTIA EVALUATION

You can dramatically improve the odds of getting a good initial evaluation by being prepared and proactive. Use this worksheet to help you gather the information the doctors need to properly evaluate your parent. You can also print and bring this list with you to an appointment. See RESOURCES.

WHAT YOU'LL WANT TO FIND OUT
FROM THIS EVALUATION

The bottom line is that you're looking for answers as to what's going on medically, what might be causing the changes you're seeing, and what the doctor proposes to do next. These answers are critical to guiding your next steps. Don't be satisfied with, "She's okay, considering her age," or at the other extreme, "There's nothing we can do."

You might be thinking that all you want is a diagnosis. It's reasonable to want this. But it's worth repeating: The first visit almost never concludes with a health provider being able to give a diagnosis. Nevertheless, you can still ask some questions to make sure things are moving toward getting one.

You'll want to especially press for answers to the following questions:

- **What might be causing the symptoms you're concerned about?**

   Doctors will generally want to get test results and try a few things before giving a definitive diagnosis. In lieu of giving a diagnosis, at the end of an initial visit, they still should be able to walk you through the possible causes they're considering. For cognitive impairment, it's quite common for there to be multiple potential causes and contributors. It can be helpful to pinpoint whether something like vision or balance seems to be a key concern and why, and what condition(s) might contribute, for example.

- **Does it appear that any medications or other common contributors to cognitive impairment are an issue?**

  Because so many medications cause worrisome effects (and because so many older adults take multiple medications), this is especially important to explore. We have a list of medications that can affect thinking in the Better Health While Aging article, "Medications known to impair brain function." See RESOURCES.

- **What can be done to stabilize or improve your parent's memory, thinking, or other aspects of their health?**

  Beyond exploring "why" questions, the doctor can help you figure out what to do about symptoms, even before a cause is pinpointed. Try to get specific suggestions for concerns that you and the exam have identified.

- **What additional tests or evaluation does the doctor think is needed, and why?**

  Usually basic labs will be ordered and often some head imaging. Some additional cognitive testing may be advised. If the initial evaluation is by a primary care doctor, he or she may want to refer your parent to neurology.

- **What is the plan for follow-up and what happens next?**

  Be sure to ask what the doctor is recommending you try right now and to come away with a clear understanding about next steps and when you'll be meeting again.

  Again, the doctor may be unable or unwilling to give you a definitive diagnosis right off the bat. They will often want to wait to get the results of lab tests and other studies. Or they may want to reevaluate your parent after making changes to medications. Getting to the bottom of dementia-like symptoms, as we've noted, can take some time because dementia symptoms can have many causes and there's no single test to confirm Alzheimer's.

Important if you've been concerned about safety issues: If you've been worried about whether your parent should be doing any particular things, like driving or managing finances, it's a good idea to ask the health provider to specifically weigh in on this question. You might want to ask (perhaps privately) if the doctor thinks your parent has the capacity to drive, manage finances, or manage other important responsibilities.

DOWNLOADABLE CHEATSHEET: IS IT DEMENTIA? THE 5 KEY FACTORS USED TO MAKE A DIAGNOSIS

This cheatsheet summarizes how doctors make a diagnosis of dementia. Use this to help you understand what a doctor needs to consider in deciding whether dementia is the actual cause of your parent's cognitive symptoms.

AFTER THE EXAM: WHAT NEXT

Some next steps will flow logically from the results of the evaluation. The following sections walk you through some things that ideally should be done at this point.

You should also know, though, that sometimes it can be hard to know how to proceed from here. Two main reasons this may be the case:

1. **It's really common for the results of an initial cognitive impairment evaluation to be ambiguous.** Although in theory it's possible to diagnose Alzheimer's in the doctor's office with upwards of 90 percent accuracy, most real-world evaluations end in uncertainty. Maybe the person has dementia, maybe not. This is often because to make an accurate diagnosis, the clinician needs information on how a person's abilities have changed over time and on how bad the functional difficulties are. Sometimes this reflects the skill of the physician. Some-

times things need time to declare themselves. This may be frustrating, but in the meantime, there are usually steps you can take to help reinforce safety or to help your parent achieve a desired goal, like remaining in their home.

2. **Sometimes a person's mental capacities are ambiguous.**
"Capacity" refers to a person's mental ability to make a given decision (or manage a certain type of task) for themselves. Sometimes the person does seem impaired and likely has mild dementia. But that doesn't mean they've automatically already lost the capacity to drive or make certain decisions, for example. So the next steps become less than clear-cut.

In fact, it's really important to know that the vast majority of people with cognitive impairment go through a "gray area" period, in which their capacity to make a variety of decisions (or do things like drive and manage finances) is borderline. It's kind of like that dawn and dusk time—a time of transition between two states. During this period, even experienced experts will find it hard to say whether the person is able to manage a specific task or decision. How long people remain in this stage is variable but if the problem actually is underlying dementia, it's common for this transitional period to last for several months or even a few years. This often makes it hard to know what should be done.

If you're like many caring adult children we know, you'd like to do all you proactively can to keep your parent safe, especially if the medical evaluation and your observations suggest worsening mental abilities. At the same time, it's important to know that unless it seems quite clear that your parent has lost capacity (more on that in Chapter 4), at this point they'll generally have the right to keep making whatever decisions they've been making, as well as a right to autonomy that deserves respect. All that said, in the meantime there may still be some middle ground or workarounds you can negotiate with your older parent.

These factors show why helping an older parent can involve so many repeated attempts.

(Ideally…) Take Measures as Needed to Address Function, Safety

Whether the diagnosis is definitely dementia, possible dementia, or something else, it's a good idea to take some basic steps that shore up your parent's well-being and function. Ideally, you'll do this in ways that support whatever goals or priorities are important to them.

Remember, most older people value financial stability (a sense of security), living where they've been, independence in decision-making or mobility (like driving), and privacy. These desires are often at odds with what their families see as urgent needs, like stopping what they perceive as a risky behavior (climbing ladders, shoveling snow, driving) and starting more protective measures (reducing clutter, sharing bill-paying, using a walker).

The specifics in your case will depend on the kinds of issues you've identified and how insistent or amenable your parent is. Generally, it's good to focus your efforts in these two categories:

1. **Develop a plan to assist with "function."** This means supporting your parent in addressing whatever daily life tasks or abilities that they need to live their best life.

2. **Address glaring safety issues.** You won't be able to make the person perfectly safe. But two particular safety issues are fairly common and warrant special attention: finances and driving.

IDENTIFY THE MOST IMPORTANT ISSUES TO ADDRESS

It's impractical to try to do everything at once. Start by determining the highest priorities. Based on your assessments, and maybe what a medical evaluation uncovered, are there immediate fixes you can address?

You'll want to quickly tackle what strikes you as most urgent. If nothing seems critical, or if you want to get momentum going, you might also start with some "low-hanging fruit"—issues that seem easy to address without too much friction or time.

CONSIDER ENLISTING EXPERT HELP

If you're unsure exactly where to begin, you might consider asking an expert for input. This is one area where outside expertise can help you make quicker progress than you might on your own. An aging life care specialist (also called a geriatric care manager) is an eldercare professional who is usually a nurse or social worker specializing in geriatrics and trained to work with families. To find one, you can try the Aging Life Care Association's Expert Search, a directory of members. You can also check with your local Area Agency on Aging office (find it with the Eldercare Locator) to see what other resources might be available in your area. (For links to all the organizations mentioned, see RESOURCES.)

OTHER STARTING PLACES FOR HELP
WITH COMMON SAFETY CONCERNS

To assess driving skills or encourage a risky driver to give up the keys

- **Can you invite your parent to take a self-assessment?** The AAA Foundation for Traffic Safety offers a Drivers 65+ self-evaluation online with suggestions for improving driving or getting further testing. If your parent has had accidents, this may be a way into the conversation.

- **Can you mention your concerns to your parent's doctor?** The provider may be willing to have this conversation with your parent or report your parent to the DMV (thus relieving you of being "the bad guy").

- **Can you arrange a driving evaluation?** Look for a driving skills evaluator or an occupational therapist driving rehabilitation specialist (OT-DRS).

- **Can you report your parent to the DMV yourself?** Check your state's Department of Motor Vehicles website to find out how the reporting of unsafe drivers works in your state. Many state DMV websites offer specific information about older drivers.

- **Can you begin to research alternate transportation?** Having a "Plan B" can make someone more amendable, so start to think about how your parent would get around, including friend/family drivers, drive services (private or from senior services), public transport options, Uber/Lyft/SilverRide, and so on.

- **If you think your parent is an immediate danger on the road, you can also consider alerting the police.**

For specific sources of help in addressing driving concerns, see RE-SOURCES.

To help safeguard finances

- **Can you begin to assemble a list of all your parent's financial accounts and documents?** Your parent may be willing to tell you where they store key papers and possibly access information. At minimum, he or she may be open to your helping to organize where things stand and do things like automate certain payments and look for recurring payments (subscriptions, memberships) or credit cards that can be canceled.

- **Can you find out whether your parent has assigned a power of attorney for finances or begin steps to become that person?** You may want to consult an elder law attorney. You'll also want to identify any existing relationships your parent has with accountants, brokers, financial advisers, or attorneys, if they'll share that information.

- **If you think your parent is losing a lot of money right now or being exploited (theft, abuse), you'll have to look into op-**

tions for taking immediate protective action. For instance, you might need to notify law enforcement or Adult Protective Services. If you have legal authority (see next chapter), you'll want to take steps to manage accounts. The next chapter also describes what you can do if you don't have legal standing to make decisions on your parent's behalf.

For specific good sources of help on safeguarding finances, see RE-SOURCES.

To reduce obvious hazards in the home

- **Can you get help evaluating what the particular risks are in your parent's home?** An occupational therapist or physical therapist can do a Home Safety Evaluation to help you identify ways to address specific needs. Medicare may cover part or all of the cost of this service for someone who has been recently discharged from the hospital or needs home care. A certified aging-in-place specialist (CAPS) is a designation from the National Association of Home Builders and AARP for trained builders who can recommend structural home modifications.

- **Are there simple fixes you can suggest or make that are more likely to be agreed to?** These might include removing clutter, loose cords, and other fall hazards, or replacing a toilet with a taller model.

For more specific sources of help on reducing home hazards, see RE-SOURCES.

What you can do about other immediate safety concerns

If you believe your parent is in immediate danger at home—for example, is acting uncontrollably and you're alarmed—you can call 911, the police, or Adult Protective Services (APS). In these cases, the person may be taken to the emergency room or treated as a psychiatric emergency. But this is an emergency, short-term fix, of course.

Bear in mind that for most concerns, even serious ones, remedies take time. It's not that we don't wish it were possible to get a properly equipped crisis team in to help you with a quick, urgent phone call. But at this time, the best we have is Adult Protective Services, a social services program (run by state or local governments) to serve at-risk older adults and those with disabilities. Sometimes they can organize a plan of local services to help someone who refuses all other help. But APS is underfunded and far from a panacea.

(Ideally...) Continue Working With the Doctors to Treat Any Treatable/Reversible Causes of Cognitive Dysfunction

Most often in cases of suspected cognitive decline, the problem is a form of progressive dementia caused by damage to brain neurons. This damage comes from injury (such as some traumatic brain injury), blood-vessel damage from a stroke or cerebral small vessel disease, (which causes vascular dementia), or most commonly, a neurodegenerative condition (the most common ones are Alzheimer's, Lewybody disease, Parkinson's disease, and frontotemporal degeneration).

Not all cognitive symptoms are caused by dementia, however. If the doctor finds that another cause may be to blame, the first thing you want to do is address that. Troubles with memory, thinking skills, or other behaviors may significantly improve, or even disappear, with treatment. That's another reason having a cognitive evaluation can be life changing. (Note that it's also possible for dementia to coexist with some of these things or more than one factor may be contributing to symptoms.)

Be sure to get clear medical guidance about how these diagnoses should be treated.

Even in someone who already has permanent brain changes due to dementia, it's extremely common for thinking skills to be worse than they could be because of other factors. Medications, especially, can exacerbate symptoms. So can other unaddressed issues, including certain vitamin deficiencies and hormonal imbalances. Addressing these factors can improve symptoms.

To find out more, see the article in RESOURCES: "10 Common causes of cognitive impairment."

(Ideally...) Take Practical Steps to Help Your Parent's Thinking Be at its Best

Non-drug approaches that support brain function and brain health can help the brain operate at its best, no matter one's age. This is even true in older adults who have cognitive impairment. Many of these are considered "lifestyle changes" and, as such, may not be brought up by doctors unless you ask about them. That said, some of these recommendations do require the help of health professionals, and some doctors, such as geriatricians, will be proactive about addressing them.

Among the areas to consider:

- **Can you discourage the use of mind-altering medications or substances?**

  In addition to drug changes the doctor may recommend, can you swap out brain-compromising over-the-counter medications for safer alternatives or use them only as a last resort? Can you persuade your parent to drink less alcohol or smoke less pot? Go to RESOURCES for a list of medications known to affect brain function.

- **Can you improve sleep?**

  Chronic sleep deprivation and insomnia contribute to poor thinking and unstable moods. Untreated disorders like sleep apnea, restless legs syndrome, and anxiety are major sleep disruptors. If your parent complains of poor sleep or being constantly fatigued, can you have a doctor look into these symptoms? (People with sleep apnea often think they've been sleeping but can't stay awake by day.) If these problems have been diagnosed, is there room for improvement in how they're being managed?

Worth noting: You'll want to be proactive about pursuing non-drug approaches. Why? Because almost all sedatives and sleeping pills will make your parent's brain function worse. Yet the average doctor still tends to resort to a prescription to treat insomnia in older adults. Know that studies show that non-drug approaches to improving insomnia are effective in older adults; some have even been developed specifically for people with dementia. So be sure to ask about those.

If your parent already feels he or she needs sedatives or sleeping pills to fall asleep: Might it be possible to wean off or at least bring down the dose? Studies show that older adults *can* successfully transition off tranquilizers.

- **Can you address social issues, like isolation or loneliness?**

  This can be a surprising source of compromised brain health. If you don't think your parent interacts often with others, can you figure out what's in the way (lack of transportation, friends moving away)? Could you hire an elder companion (from a homecare services company) or enlist regular volunteers to visit your parent or help them get out of the house?

- **Can you do anything else to help reduce stress and help your parent function their best?**

  Is your parent stressed by changes in vision or hearing or mobility that you can help address? Does your parent eat poorly, either because he or she doesn't cook, can't get to the store to buy fresh foods, or maybe has lifelong bad habits? Can you look into having meals delivered (by Meals on Wheels, a neighbor, or a delivery service)? Can you shop for your parent to help them inch more toward a Mediterranean-style diet (the kind shown to be one of the most brain- and heart-friendly)?

DOWNLOADABLE CHEATSHEET: HOW TO PROMOTE BRAIN HEALTH & EMOTIONAL HEALTH

Here you'll find some of the information in this chapter and more. In fact, it's a good idea to apply this healthy-aging advice to yourself as well, in order to possibly prevent or minimize the issues you see in your parent now.

(Ideally...) if a Diagnosis of MCI, Alzheimer's, or Other Dementia Is Made, Begin Key Support Planning

If a diagnosis of dementia (or probable dementia) is made, it's smart to be proactive about what's likely ahead. We know it's hard for most people to plan for "what ifs." Most of us tend to react rather than be proactive. But in the case of progressive dementias, we're talking less about "what ifs" than about "whens." You'll make things much easier on both you and your parent by, as early as possible, shifting to preparing for the future. The person's mental functioning *will* get worse. (Not all mild cognitive impairment advances to dementia, but since you won't know until that happens, you're back to best being prepared.)

That said, this is a BIG topic. You'll find it useful to turn to a full book just on this subject to help you prepare. One to try: Paula's *Surviving Alzheimer's: Practical Tips and Soul-Saving Wisdom for Caregivers*, which walks readers through all the basics and covers advice from doctors (including Dr. K), social workers, psychologists, and other experts and family caregivers.

You'll want to explore the steps described earlier in the chapter to support safety and function and to optimize cognitive function. In addition, here's a very brief overview of just some of what families need to address specific to a new dementia diagnosis:

Start learning dementia caregiving strategies. It's not too early, even if symptoms are mild. The main things to learn early on are how to communicate more effectively, ways to minimize stress and maximize independence, and how to manage common behavioral issues. If your parent has actually been given a diagnosis of dementia, then you'll also want to learn about how dementia usually progresses and what to expect over the next several years.

Address legal paperwork and advance care planning. If your parent hasn't already drawn up legal paperwork assigning powers of attorney for healthcare and finances and still seems fairly "with it" mentally, it's likely he or she still has the legal capacity to arrange them. Advance health care planning should be done in collaboration with a health professional (ideally your parent's PCP). Advance planning for finances and general affairs is often best done with an attorney (preferably one specializing in elder law). The attorney can also address a will, a financial living trust, and other issues, if they're not already in place. (The next chapter discusses these documents in detail.)

Start planning for future increased care needs. To the extent your parent will permit you, identify sources of income and savings, assets and debts. This includes reviewing any government benefits your parent may be eligible for (for medication, care, transportation, meals) including veteran's services, which can be extensive. It's also not too soon to begin researching options for when more care is needed. Even if your parent wishes to remain at home or you intend to have your parent move in with you (or vice versa), it's smart to start thinking about a series of options long before you'll need them. You don't know what the future holds, and this can be a time-consuming process.

Good resources on preparing for dementia include books, support groups, dementia care specialists, and geriatric care managers. We also have a lot on this topic at the Better Health While Aging site, including, for later reference, "7 Steps to Managing Difficult Dementia Behaviors (Safely & Without Medication." (See RESOURCES.)

Which brings us to...

(Ideally...) Start Building Up Resources and a Support Network

In addition to working with your parent's care provider, it's a good idea to spend a little time researching whatever specific care and support options might be on the table for consideration. Once you voice the problem, you'll need to be part of the solution. Having a range of possible answers ahead of time allows you to better answer your parent's questions, counter concerns, and ease both your minds about paths forward.

That's not to say you need to have everything figured out before you speak up. Offering help is ideally a collaborative thing. But by checking out possibilities in advance, you'll know more and feel better.

At the end of the book, the RESOURCES section includes a list of some of our favorite sources of help, including comprehensive books on aging and care, local and national social services and caregiving organizations, and reputable websites, including Dr. K's Better Health While Aging.

Then there are the human resources—your network for current and future help. It helps to start with a broad list of possibilities you can tap into, now or later. Among the possible sources you may be cultivating:

- Your employer's human resources or services department

- Other relatives who might be part of a solution

- Specialists in various areas

- Support services (cleaning, meals, transportation, delivery services)

- Religious groups you or your parent might belong to

- Other friends or sources of support you can think of

- Online caregiver groups (someone out there will have encountered your situation before)

Clearly, this is a lot to consider and do! We don't expect anyone to whip through everything in this chapter. That's why we keep using the word "ideally." At this point, use this information to confirm or enlarge your sense of which kinds of things most make sense, in your particular situation, for you to tackle. In Part Three, we'll guide you through choosing and implementing the specific steps.

What This Looks Like:
The Smiths and The Johnsons

Example 1: The Smiths

Zeke Smith felt overwhelmed when his evaluation of his father's situation confirmed that Albert really needed help, though he didn't think he did. After Zeke got back to his siblings about where things stood, his sister was willing to take some action to help their father. His brother still seemed uninterested but once presented with a list of what's been going on, did also agree that something would eventually need to change.

Here's where they stood:

- They felt they really needed to know if their father's longtime doctor, whom they know he sees regularly, shared their concern about Albert's memory and judgment. Had he noticed? Had any kind of diagnosis been made? How could they get this information, if Albert wasn't willingly sharing it?

- They also wanted to address his driving. It didn't seem safe. How could they be sure, or convince him to take the accidents more seriously? Could they find alternatives for him to get around, maybe the neighbors to drive him for groceries or getting him used to a ride service?

- Then there were the financial worries. If their dad was writing big, unnecessary checks to neighbors, might he be doing more of that? Was he at risk of financial exploitation? How could they keep his money safer?

Since Zeke had springing power of attorney for healthcare and finances, he wondered how and when he should take steps to activate them. And he still wondered about getting Albert on board with any kinds of changes.

Learning the next steps that should ideally happen in their situation gave them a starting place for how to think about what should happen next.

Ideally, they would:

- Find out whether Albert's doctor is aware of Albert's memory issues and what, if anything, he's done so far.

- Get Albert's cognitive symptoms medically evaluated.

- Look into the springing powers of attorney for healthcare and finances, and meanwhile see what steps can be taken now to address Albert's driving difficulties and to protect him from financial mismanagement.

- Check Albert's medications against a list they found of medications that can make memory and thinking worse.

- Learn more about communicating with a parent who's having memory problems, since this seems to be an issue they'll be dealing with for the next several months, if not indefinitely.

Now how to actually get this done? They weren't quite sure. But at least now they had a clearer idea of what to aim for.

Example 2: The Johnsons

For Sue Johnson, thinking about the "ideal" way to help her mother clarified the need to confirm something she'd begun to wonder about: Was it "just grief" behind her forgetfulness and other mental slipping or was something wrong? Maria hated doctors and, as far as Sue knew, hadn't been to see one in years. But this seemed to be the best starting point. How could she get her there?

She also saw that by tackling some key functions and safety issues, she could help her mom manage better so that she, Sue, might worry less.

She made a quick list of ideal next steps to work on, based on what she'd learned:

- Look into options for getting Maria a medical evaluation for cognitive impairment and for depression. Even though she knows it will be hard to actually get her mother to a health provider, Sue decides to see what's available in their area, maybe her own doctor? She also considers whether to consult with a geriatric care manager, both because these professionals know which health providers are available locally and because she'd read they often have experience in getting reluctant older people to a doctor.

- To address the safety issues related to the stove, research and see what kind of stove alarms or shutoffs might be available. She feels relieved that her mother is otherwise accepting her help.

- To help her mom's cognitive function be its best, focus on routines and minimizing her mom's stress when possible. She also decides to try to schedule Maria to have time with her friends. She wonders if her aunt, who has been dismissive about the memory issues, might help her do this and also, by spending more time with her sister, observe the cognitive concerns more closely. Sue also goes through her mother's medicine cabinet with a list of common OTC meds that aren't recommended for people with memory problems and gets rid of the Tylenol PM.

- Spend some time seeing if she can encourage her mom to complete some power of attorney documents.

- Find out more on helpful ways of communicating with a parent with memory problems.

- Find out more about grief support groups, in case this was the underlying problem for Maria.

Chapter 4:
Realize Why the Ideal Is Usually Hard
(Here's What You Can Do)

Your family dynamics might be such that your parent is open to communicating what's going on and responsive to whatever you suggest to improve the situation—and no one else will object or intrude. If so, congratulations. That's the ideal. But you're probably reading this book because things aren't going so smoothly. Or, perhaps, no matter how it's going now, you're unsure how things might change.

In reality, the commonsensical steps outlined in the previous chapter tend to be harder to pull off than families expect. Common problems include:

- Your parent refuses to go to the doctor.

- Your parent refuses to discuss the situation with you (or with others).

- Your parent might be getting more paranoid and/or accusing you of certain motives.

- Your parent or their partner won't allow you to help address function or safety issues.

- Conversations tend to turn into fights or stony silences.

- You're unsure of how you can insist that your parent get a needed evaluation or make a necessary change.

- You feel like you're facing impossible situations where all available options stink.

Why do these issues come up? It's partly due to the fact that you and your parent are two different individuals, each with a unique way of seeing a situation and, probably, differing (sometimes clashing) goals and priorities. You each do things in your own way.

Most families are also getting tripped up by at least one—if not both—of the following:

1. **Mental capacity issues,** which can affect how competent an older person is to make certain decisions (and understand the related risks and likely consequences).

2. **Communication issues,** which can cause your well-intentioned efforts to go nowhere...or even to backfire.

These are two extremely common, major reasons that families have difficulty helping an older person to get the evaluation they need and/or to accept more help and support.

In this chapter, we'll explain what you need to know about recognizing—and addressing—these issues.

When There Are Mental Capacity Concerns

In the United States, adults have a fundamental right to individual autonomy, which means they're allowed to make decisions and take actions that family members may not like.

But there's a big exception to the right to autonomy, especially in situations where cognition is worrisome: the person making a decision has to have the mental capacity to understand what's going on and to make reasonably informed decisions.

If a person is lacking this mental capacity to understand their situation and the likely consequences of their actions, then it becomes ethically permissible to intervene.

(It then also becomes even more important to be thoughtful about how you communicate; more on that in the next section.)

What to Know About Capacity (and Competence)

"Capacity" has slightly different meanings to doctors and lawyers, but generally it's whether a person has the capability to make a decision—that is, can they demonstrate that they have the mental abilities to do so? Generally, capacity requires that an individual be able to understand:

- The situation they're in

- The decision in question

- The consequences of a given choice

(Historically, the term "capacity" was used more by health professionals and the terms "competence" and "incompetent" were used more to describe a legal determination. However, legal professionals have been moving toward using the term "capacity" as well.)

Contrary to what some people think, decisional capacity isn't an all-or-nothing, they-can-or-they-can't state. It's actually supposed to be situation-dependent.

There are many different kinds of capacity. Among those that might be relevant to an older adult: financial capacity, medical consent capacity, testamentary capacity (the legal and mental ability to make a will), capacity to drive, capacity to live independently, and sexual consent capacity.

Specific legal standards for capacity vary by state law. But it's always supposed to be decision-specific. That means capacity should be evaluated in terms of a particular decision at hand. A person might not be capable of making a complex decision (like sorting through the tax consequences of selling a property) but still able to make simpler ones (like deciding whether to take a medication).

What's more, capacity can fluctuate. Someone may not have capacity immediately following surgery but be fine a week later. Or someone with dementia will have good days and bad days, especially early on. It's possible for sleep and rest, good care, hearing aids or wearing glasses, and other factors to improve someone's capacity. That said, over the course of a progressive brain-damaging condition such as Alzheimer's disease, capacity for most kinds of decisions disappears.

A health provider's capacity assessment is often used by legal professionals to guide their actions. For instance, durable power of attorney documents may specify that the agent's authority becomes active when one (or sometimes two) physicians declare someone incapacitated.

Such capacity assessments and declarations can potentially be done by a primary care physician but they may not be comfortable doing so. And honestly, very few of them have been adequately trained for this purpose. For instance, a doctor asked to check for capacity (or "competence") should find out the particular reason it's for and then write a specific conclusion, with documentation. Experts also recommend that health providers document the likely reason that capacity is impaired and whether they expect it to be permanent or not.

Unfortunately, this isn't how it's usually done. Many doctors will simply write a blanket summary like, "Mrs. So-and-So has lost her mental capacity." This may or may not have any legal standing. (A key telltale sign: when asked about their patient's capacity, they should ask "capacity to do what?"—but most don't.)

Psychologists, geriatricians, and certain specially trained clinicians are usually better at assessing capacity. Families, of course, make decisions based on these assessments (or even just based on their own informal assessment) all the time. It's often not a problem until someone else contests the action in court.

WHY YOUR PARENT'S CAPACITY MATTERS

If you've been worried about your aging parent's actions or decisions or frustrated because they won't pursue the "ideal" approach, it's crucial to consider the question of whether they have capacity.

That's because legally and ethically, we don't have the right to interfere in other people's affairs, unless it seems they have lost the capacity to understand their decisions and actions.

IF YOUR PARENT HAS CAPACITY...

- You might continue to be worried about their well-being and feel uncomfortable with the choices they're making. In fact, the things they choose to do might strike you as unsafe, unwise, inconvenient, terrible, or ridiculous. (What we hear a lot: "He's so stubborn." "She insists on doing risky things." "They never listen.") If your parents are of sound mind, though, they get to make those choices. Unless or until things change, you'll need to find ways to live comfortably with those decisions, even if that's a sucky feeling.

- You do get to continue to help, encourage, suggest, research, and plan, or even pressure your parent to make changes you feel are in his or her best interest. Whether or not you push, or how hard, depends on factors like how much danger you think they are to themselves or others and how willing you are to live with their being upset with you (also a potentially sucky feeling).

- Your parent's doctor can only communicate directly with you about your parent's condition if your parent has consented to this, either verbally or by signing the provider's release. (You can still express concerns or report symptoms to the doctor but privacy rules prevent them from disclosing case information to you.)

IF YOUR PARENT DOESN'T HAVE CAPACITY...

- You can begin to make decisions on your parent's behalf if he or she has legal tools already in place (such as a power of attorney for finances or healthcare) that name you as having such authority in this event. Alternately, if it's not you, you can work with the person who has been named proxy, such as a sibling or spouse.

- Your parent's doctor will have more wiggle room to communicate directly with you about your parent's condition, whether or not you have power of attorney. Privacy laws allow providers some flexibility in disclosing case information without the patient's permission if they believe doing so is in the best interests of someone they believe to be lacking capacity. (You can read a description of this allowance in the Better Health While Aging article, "10 things to know about HIPAA and access to a relative's health information;" go to RESOURCES.)

- You can put changes in place to help your parent, even those he or she might not be crazy about, with a greater sense of ethical confidence (and possibly less guilt), knowing that you're acting in their best interests.

IF IT'S UNCLEAR WHETHER YOUR PARENT HAS CAPACITY...

This is a fairly common situation. It can come up because an older person hasn't yet been evaluated. Or, even after an evaluation, a person may be in a "gray area" when it comes to decision-making and judgment for such common life situations as managing finances, driving, or assessing a living situation.

If this seems to be your situation:

- Society generally gives the older person the benefit of the doubt unless it's quite clear they are incapacitated. This means you'll generally need to err on the side of allowing your parent to make their decisions, even if you're worried or uncomfortable.

As noted above, you can still try to influence them.

- You can continue to try to bring your concerns to the attention of those in a position to evaluate your parent (e.g. your parent's health provider) or to address risky situations (e.g. Adult Protective Services).

What to Know About Powers of Attorney and Other Legal Documents That Can Help You

If you think your parent is losing the ability to make certain decisions on their behalf, you'll want to check ASAP to see if he or she has previously completed any legal documents or other authorizations that can enable you to more easily assist or intervene. They fall into two main categories:

1. **Documents and authorizations related to healthcare**. These include the durable power of attorney for healthcare and "HIPAA releases."

2. **Documents and authorizations related to finances and general affairs**. These include the durable general power of attorney and living trusts.

For any document or authorization, you'll want to look closely to see if there's a condition that the principal (that's the person completing the document) must be declared incapacitated before someone else is authorized to assist or act on their behalf.

These are sometimes called "springing" powers of attorney because they only "spring" into action once incapacity has been declared. Such "springing" documents usually specify how incapacity will be determined. (This is yet another example of why it's so important to consider capacity issues!)

These types of legal documents and authorizations are governed by state laws but the general principles of how they work is broadly similar in most states.

Here's how these documents can be used as you strive to help your parent:

DOCUMENTS AND AUTHORIZATIONS FOR HEALTHCARE

A durable power of attorney for healthcare (DPOAH) allows a person to designate a "surrogate" decision maker, which means an agent who can make healthcare decisions on their behalf.

This is often included as part of a larger "advance healthcare directive," which may also include guidance on what kind of medical care one would or wouldn't want, if one were too sick to make one's own medical decisions.

Like many POA documents, a DPOAH document usually includes a box in which the principal (that's the person completing the document) indicates whether the agent's authority is effective immediately versus only if the principal is deemed incapacitated.

The main thing to know, if you are named in your parent's DPOAH document, is that when your authority is effective, you have the right to request medical records and communicate with your parent's health providers. Federal law essentially says that healthcare surrogates have the same right to information as the principal.

This means that having a currently effective DPOAH can enable you to get medical information from your parent's providers and allows the providers to communicate with you.

A related, but more limited authorization, is a *"HIPAA authorization" or "HIPAA release."* (Pronounced "HIP-pah," the acronym comes from the Health Insurance Portability and Accountability Act which established standards for privacy.) These are authorizations created by health providers to document that a patient is authorizing the health provider to disclose information to specific other people. Interestingly, the HIPAA Privacy Rule itself doesn't mandate use of these written releases, but it's very common for health providers to use them and honor them.

A HIPAA release will generally give you fewer options than a DPOAH. But it can still be convenient if you have one, as it will make it easier for your parent's health provider to communicate with you regarding your concerns.

For more on HIPAA, see "10 things to know about HIPAA and access to a relative's health info" in RESOURCES.

Note: You may be wondering about a "living will." This term refers to a document that specifies a person's medical preferences if one is too sick or incapacitated to make decisions. It doesn't usually give someone actual legal authority to make decisions, although it can contain useful guidance for family members and health providers. If you've heard your parent has a "living will," don't assume it includes a power of attorney unless you've looked it over carefully.

DOCUMENTS AND AUTHORIZATIONS RELATED TO FINANCES AND GENERAL AFFAIRS

A *durable general power of attorney* allows the named agent to transact business and otherwise make specific decisions on the principal's behalf, even if they become incapacitated.

People often set up a non-springing version to enable a trusted person to help out when it's convenient or to have an extra set of eyes on financial decisions. Or they can set up a "springing" version so that others will be able to access their financial accounts and transact business if the principal is ever sick or otherwise incapacitated.

A durable general power of attorney doesn't give carte-blanche to make decisions for someone or to override their decisions so long as they're able.

But you will definitely have more options when it comes to addressing your parent's financial affairs if you have a durable general power of attorney, especially if it's the non-springing type.

A *living trust* is another legal tool that can enable family members to step in and assist. Living trusts are created to hold financial assets, which are managed by one or more trustees. Initially, the trustee is often the person whose assets are in the trust and that person is also the beneficiary of the trust. Trust documents generally include a provision explaining who will become the "successor trustee," if the original trustee is incapacitated.

If your parents have put any assets in a trust, you'll want to find out who is the successor trustee and what are the conditions for control passing to a successor.

How to Get a "Springing" Power of Attorney Activated

A common question that families have is, "How do I get a springing power of attorney 'activated?'"

The power of attorney document itself will specify how incapacity is to be determined. For instance, it might say that two physicians have to attest to incapacity in writing.

For the power of attorney to be accepted as valid, families will generally need to provide whatever proof of incapacity is specified, along with the power of attorney, to the party you're transacting business with (e.g. a title company, utility, and so on).

In most states, "activation" is not something that is declared by an attorney or by a judge.

From a practical perspective, the biggest challenge families often encounter is that an incapacitated older adult may well refuse to see a doctor or otherwise cooperate with an evaluation of their capacity. There are ways around this common obstacle; we'll cover them in the next chapter.

IF YOUR PARENT HASN'T NAMED YOU (OR ANYONE ELSE) IN A POWER OF ATTORNEY DOCUMENT

If this is the case, your options to help or intervene will be more limited, unless your parent is able—and willing—to go ahead and complete a POA.

It's certainly worthwhile to see if this can happen. Of course, you'll want to consult with a lawyer—and potentially also a health provider—to see if your parent still has the capacity to complete a POA and name an agent. This is often still possible in the early (and sometimes even moderate) stages of dementia because ability fluctuates. The lawyer is required by law and ethical codes to make an informal assessment of whether the person seems competent to complete the legal task at hand. For example, they might ask a few questions about the date and the purpose of the visit to gauge mental competence. (Note: This is different from a clinical assessment made by medical personnel, which is generally more detailed and looks for the medical reason behind compromised capacity.) Try to make an appointment on a day and time (typically in the morning, after a good sleep) when your parent is at his or her best.

Legal experts often advise that a non-springing durable power of attorney is more practical than a springing one because it's more clear-cut. It takes effect immediately and you don't need to provide proof that the person is incapacitated. The biggest downside is that a person may not feel the degree of trust that such a document requires and therefore be less willing to choose this option. (Of note, the American Bar Association recently suggested some additional protections that can be drafted into the power of attorney, such as requiring third-party accounting to reduce the risk of abuse; learn more in RESOURCES: "Reducing the risk of power of attorney abuse" podcast.)

To arrange a POA, look for a family law attorney, especially one who specializes in elder law. Yes, this is an expense. But it's a cost-effective step that can spare you time and grief down the road, so well worth the investment. We've seen it again and again, in all kinds of families, how having proper basic documents in place makes everything easier.

It's always a good idea to check with an attorney rather than just making your own assessment of competence or relying on what the doctor has said. That's because any decisions without this step can put you on shaky legal and ethical ground.

If someone other than you (like your parent's spouse or a sibling) has been named to have the legal authority to make decisions, you'll need to work with that person to effect the changes you want to see.

If a lawyer determines your parent is unable to arrange a power of attorney because mental ability is waning, you can try returning on a different day, given that capacity can fluctuate in early cognitive decline. But if it's too late, the primary other legal option for taking action on your parent's financial affairs and for overriding their decisions, especially those that put them in financial jeopardy or put their safety at risk, is guardianship (also known as conservatorship in some states).

What to Know About
Guardianship/Conservatorship

This tool is used when there is no power of attorney or living trust in place for an adult who has become incapacitated and can obviously no longer manage his or her own affairs.

The process and criteria for qualifying for guardianship vary from state to state, but in general, someone (often a concerned family member like you) must petition the court to have the person declared incapacitated and in need of guardianship. (In some places this is referred to as conservatorship.) In some cases, Adult Protective Services may initiate the guardianship petition, if they have become involved in the older person's case and are concerned enough. After a review of evidence, if the court agrees that the person is incapacitated and in need of guardianship, the court transfers responsibility to you (the petitioner) or to another party for the person's finances, living arrangements, healthcare decisions, and related tasks. There can be a conservator just for the estate, if needed (if, say, the person already has advance directives about healthcare) or just for the person (if, say, there's a power of attorney for finances in place), or for both.

"Getting guardianship" can be a complicated and expensive process. You need to hire a lawyer and appear in court. It gets tricky if families disagree about who should be the guardian or whether one is needed at all. It can also be fraught if your parent is resistant and still able to make certain decisions or lacks insight into his or her changing mental abilities (which is common); guardianship can feel humiliating.

Still, in some cases it's the only way to effectively intervene to help your parent with health, finances, housing, or safety issues.

Before it comes to that, it's important to consider all the other approaches at your disposal, which the following chapters cover. These can include:

- Using persuasion and collaboration with your parent and other stakeholders in their life to set up health, safety, and independence measures that at least temporarily shore up the situation.

- Working with an outside professional to achieve a (possibly temporary) improvement in the situation, such as a social worker experienced in eldercare or a geriatric care manager.

- Calling Adult Protective Services in the event you're getting nowhere and suspect self-neglect. (See Chapter 6 for more about this.)

If you find yourself in a situation where you need to consider guardianship, it's smart to start by consulting a reputable local geriatric care manager who has been involved in guardianship cases. You will eventually need to consult with a good attorney but starting with an attorney can be expensive. An experienced geriatric care manager, on the other hand, will be familiar with the local landscape of family or probate courts and local judges. Different courts can have very different standards for granting guardianship. The threshold is usually, but not always, high. These cases are subject both to local jurisdictions and state laws. (In one state, for example, if a petition for guardianship fails, the petitioner has to pay all the court costs and can't try again for two years—information important to understand in advance!)

In addition to giving you a more affordable down-low on what the courts in your area look like, a geriatric care manager can provide valuable advice on how you can prepare for this possibility or suggest other things you can try to avoid this drastic step.

To find the right person, you might need to ask around. Start with local or virtual caregiving groups to network around. Of course, an elder law attorney can also provide the legal insights, although it may cost more.

Now that we've covered the basics of mental capacity issues and the related legal concepts, let's move on to the second big obstacle that often makes it hard to pursue the ideal plan: communication issues.

How Communication Builds or Blocks Progress

Whatever you choose to do, it's enormously useful to get your parent (and possibly others) on board. Good communication skills, even if they don't come naturally to you, are about more than niceties: they can make the difference between discord and satisfaction, or between stalemate and accomplishment.

In fact—and here's why we're making such a big deal about this—**how you interact and communicate is one of two main aspects to helping an older parent entirely within your control.** (How you research and choose options is the other one.)

Think about it. You can't control your parent's condition. You can't control his or her reactions to your ideas. You really can't control the outcome of the situation, no matter how much careful planning, energy, thought, or cash you put into it.

What is entirely within your power, however, is how you choose to engage with your parent (and key others) about the situation. What you say, how you say it, and when you say it, can reduce resistance and other conflicts and encourage agreement and cooperation.

Even when your parent has cognitive impairment or lacks capacity in certain regards, you'll do yourselves both a huge favor by communicating with respect and sensitivity.

These basic guidelines encourage the momentum you want:

COMMUNICATING TO REDUCE CONFLICT
AND ENHANCE COOPERATION

Stay curious about, and open to, your parent's perspective. It's their life, after all. By keeping the focus on how *they* see the problem or how *they* feel about possible improvements, you'll help them feel heard, validated, and respected. This will increase the odds that they'll be willing to accept suggestions or compromise, even if you can't always arrange things as they'd like.

Invite your parent's solutions. Ask questions before making outright suggestions: "What would you like to see happen?" "How do you think yardwork should be managed now that the doctor says you should cut back?" "Do you have a better idea?" "Is there something else you think we should try first?" Then listen to the answers for any underlying concern (money, mobility, loneliness) that you can address when you pitch alternate ideas.

When talking about your own feelings or opinions, stick to "I statements." This approach, to frame your comments using the words "I" or "me," helps you avoid making accusations or sounding like you're giving orders. "What I'm worried about when I hear you say that is..." "It makes me feel upset to see that..." "I've looked into that and it seems to me that..." (What to avoid: "You statements," as in, "You keep saying..." or "You should..." or "Why don't you...?")

Frame your ideas in positives. Emphasize what's beneficial, better, cheaper, or nicer about any given suggestion. For example, "Wow, I always thought grab bars were ugly but I read this article about how now it's called 'universal design' and it's a trendy way to add value to your house." Or "This program at the center is free if you're over 65. Julie's mom is interested, would you go with her to check it out?" Steer away from pointing out losses, limitations, and inabilities.

Avoid phrases with the words *always* and *never*. Absolutes like these can make someone angry and defensive. ("You always act like that."

"You never listen to me.") Or they can lead you into promises you may not be able to keep. ("I'll never put you in a nursing home." "I'll always come when you call.")

Use empathy and validation. Above all, people want to feel that they're being heard. (Don't you?) One great communication technique that accomplishes this: Replay back to your parent what they've said, rephrasing: "So you really want to…" "Okay, I hear you saying that you're worried about…" "You're sad about the idea of…"

No matter how frustrated you get, avoid insisting, arguing, threatening, or otherwise putting your parent on the defensive. This can feel good in the moment but it's always counterproductive.

COMMUNICATING BETTER WHEN THERE ARE CONCERNS ABOUT MEMORY, THINKING, OR CAPACITY

If your parent has been showing signs of memory or thinking problems, might be mentally incapacitated, or even has a diagnosis of dementia, there are some added considerations:

Avoid arguing about what's true or real. Someone with cognitive impairment is losing the ability to see your point of view or even the reality of a situation—and that's the perfect setup for lots of disagreements. Knowing this ahead of time can help you sidestep locked horns before it happens.

Forget about insisting you can get them to "understand." Another communication issue that we see trip up families is an insistence on getting a parent on board with the reasoning and logic behind a particular decision, especially one the parent might not prefer. When cognitive issues are present, brain functions that support logic, judgment, and rationality are affected. No matter how hard you try, no matter how patient your explanations, your parent may become upset, hold a decision against you, or behave in other uncharacteristic ways. Unfortunately, this is a common aspect of living with cognitive impairment that you can't do anything about. It's natural to want to explain and it's fine to try, to a limited extent. But don't beat yourself up if doing so goes nowhere. And definitely don't persist with getting them to understand if it's not working.

Don't expect a logical flow to your conversations. Your parent may not be able to engage in thoughtful negotiations or follow lines of thinking that make perfect sense to you. Yet your autopilot impulse will be to fall back on the same logic and other ways of conversing with your parent that you've always used. Even if much of the time they seem "normal," brain changes can interfere with (or prevent) really productive, linear talks. If you find yourself feeling frustrated by your parent's lack of logic, try to take a deep breath. Then focus on listening to them and accepting where they are at with their thinking, even if it seems to be going in circles or isn't logical.

Don't feel compelled to tell the whole truth or nothing but the truth. When someone has cognitive challenges, it's okay to hide certain aspects of the truth or leave out certain facts. Really. It's also often appropriate to tell a "fiblet"—a kind of white lie sometimes called a "therapeutic non-truth"—when doing so will cause them less distress or anxiety. Think of it as suspending your natural preference to be perfectly honest at all times in service of the bigger goal of what's ultimately in your parent's best interests. This is different from deceiving someone in order to do them harm. You're doing so out of empathy and compassion to lessen their stress and improve their situation.

Help the brain's slowed processor by simplifying. You might try slowing your rate of speech a bit (not in an exaggerated way but with more patience than you might be used to). Break big ideas and long sentences into fewer words. Rather than rushing in to fill a silence, give your parent time to respond, maybe more time than you're used to.

When a conversation goes off the rails, try steering to emotions rather than facts. Instead of trying to correct or convince, play back what they seem to be feeling: "You seem upset about that." "You sound anxious about how you'll get around." When someone feels heard, you can bypass an argument or flat-out resistance. Show empathy now and revisit the topic later.

Remember that your words are just part of communication. All of us, but especially those with cognitive impairment, actually get more out of speakers' body language (frowning face, crossed arms) and tone of voice (impatience, sarcasm, insincerity). It really helps to go out of your way to do things like smile, make eye contact, gently touch a shoulder as you talk, and use a reassuring or upbeat tone.

CONSIDERING OTHER MESSENGERS

Worth considering: Are you the best person to have a particular conversation with your parent? Or might someone else make a better messenger? Sometimes the way into your parent is through their partner, a sibling, or a trusted family friend who can be particularly persuasive. In some cases, aging parents have been known to listen more to a son- or daughter-in-law than to their adult child. Should you go this route, though, try to hammer out a unified front on what your goal is so nobody feels blindsided, which can add stress instead of easing it. You might also consider whether to involve an authority figure that your parent has historically been willing to listen to, such as a trusted religious leader, a physician, an attorney, or a financial advisor.

When you're really stuck, an outsider skilled in communications regarding aging can often break a logjam. Depending on the situation, you might find it helpful for a geriatric care manager, attorney, social worker, or other aging care professional to take the lead on a particular discussion. Some family therapists and mediators have also developed expertise in helping older adults and their families navigate these conversations.

NAVIGATING FAMILY DYNAMICS AS YOU GO

Even though you'll be feeling like you have your hands full with your parent and, understandably, may feel reluctant to spend extra time communicating with other family members, now is actually an important time to optimize family communication. Why bother? Because you're all heading toward harder times. The challenges ahead are apt to stress the strongest relationships and bring out all the dysfunctions in less optimal relationships.

Connecting effectively with the other parties concerned can make the difference between more help and more stress. Some pointers to keep in mind:

Think about using similar communications strategies with siblings or other family members that you use with your parent. Invite their opinion, listen as much as you talk, empathize with their perspective, and avoid getting caught up in arguments or standoffs.

Instead of automatically viewing other family as adversaries, try to see the power in groupthink and collaborative talks. Remember that every family member has a unique relationship to your parent and things might look different from where they stand with different priorities or concerns—or new insights into workable solutions.

Keep lines of communication open and transparent among family. The reason: This helps all the stakeholders feel listened to. It can make others more inclined to help you, while also heading off conflict and making it more likely for them to get on board with your choices. That's not to sound too rosy because difficult family dynamics do occur. (See Chapter 6 on some common obstacles.)

Weigh whether it's worth enlisting third-party help. Neutral experts like a geriatric care manager, other aging-services professional, financial planner, or doctor can be helpful if you have a history of contentious relationships and expect that any efforts to help your parent might put you down a thorny path with relatives. There are also family therapists and mediators who specialize in helping families resolve eldercare conflicts.

What Else to Know About Your Roles and Goals

Whatever your parent's mental capacity and whatever the legal tools at your disposal, an ongoing struggle will be how to help your parent while preserving his or her autonomy and dignity as much as possible.

Although this may feel like the right thing to do, it can also feel like a tall order.

The burden on families in helping aging adults today is huge. There's no single silver bullet to solve most situations, no magic phone call that will make your parent safe and cared for, plus happy to accept the help. As you'll soon discover, if you haven't already, there's no well-organized "system" in place to help organize and address eldercare needs. In many areas, it's hard to even find the kinds of resources that can help.

Even when you have resources available and experts to help you navigate them, it can be an agonizing challenge to walk the line between respecting your parent's judgments or wishes and giving yourself peace of mind.

So it's important to realize: You won't always be able to help them in ways that they—or others—might like. And you won't always be able to get them the outcome that you want for them or even the outcome that they might want for themselves.

All of which is why we want to you to keep coming back to a few key ideas as you journey through this part of your parent's life:

Ultimately, this is your role in a nutshell:

- To research problems and possible ways to face them.

- To make the effort to understand your parent's preferences, priorities, goals, and desires (even if you can't always meet them).

- To consider how to proceed in light of what you've learned.

- To propose and encourage solutions in the most skillful and compassionate way you can.

- To provide emotional support to help your parent cope with whatever happens.

- To take care of yourself, to be best equipped physically, mentally, and emotionally to do all of the above.

What your role *isn't*: Your role isn't to fix everything to your satisfaction or to keep your parent as safe as possible because those goals aren't usually feasible, permanent, or possible.

- **You will periodically need to untangle what *you* need from what your parent needs.** Most of us have a natural tendency to want, or even to expect, others to "do what's good for them." Or to accept needed changes. Or we want things to stay the same forever. That's human nature. The more productive—and infinitely more peaceful—course is to accept that sometimes things are just the way they are and that we have to change ourselves (adjust our preferences, modify our expectations, let go of rigid ideas) rather than trying to force others to bend to our way.

- **There's no absolute hierarchy of what's most important in a situation.** You might think it's keeping Mom or Dad safe. But at what cost? Your parent might put a higher value on having a sense of freedom or control and be willing to accept a certain amount of risk. How a decision gets made can come down to capacity. Even then, though, deciding the priorities usually involves a fair amount of compromise all around.

- **You won't be able to control everything (or everyone) to your highest satisfaction.** Helping an older parent usually involves some degree of acceptance and letting go. This can mean settling for situations that aren't ideal or that you know are only temporary, and that might have consequences down the road for you, requiring you to "pick up the pieces" later.

- **You may need to settle for incremental progress.** Another way of looking at the point above: Winning your parent's confidence in, or acceptance of, small changes may make larger ones more possible later. Sometimes it pays to tackle relatively easy "low hanging fruit" first, even if it's only a small or temporary part of a solution.

- **You'll want to set boundaries for yourself as you go.** Unless you've been named in legal documents, your obligation to help your parent is a moral one rather than a legal one. You want to do right by your parent to the best of your ability. But you can only do what you can do.

The most realistic (and satisfying) mindset is to think of your role as accompanying your parent on a journey, to the best of your ability, rather than getting them to a particular destination.

TOOL: THE ME VS. THEM EXERCISE

If you and your parent find yourselves at loggerheads, try this thought process to help you break out of it:

1. **Give some real thought to what's motivating you.**

    What are your fears?

    What are your frustrations?

    What are your priorities in helping your parent right now?

    What would success look like to you? (What are your goals here?)

2. **Now think about the same questions the way your parent/s might answer them.** (Think about what they're saying to you now, if anything, as well as indications you might have because of ways they've acted or things they've said in the past.)

    What are they afraid of?

    What, if anything, is frustrating them?

    What are their priorities right now?

    How do you think success looks like to them? (What are their goals?)

3. **What are some major ways that your perspectives are distinct from each other?**

4. **What are ways you could let go of your preferences in order to respect your parent's preferences?** Remember that the natural human tendency is to try to get others to change (or to try to keep things from changing). For the sake of your relationship and both sides' stress levels, the more effective path is to change what you can about yourself. Could what you change be something about your approach? Could it be the solution you're aiming for? Could you change a heartfelt sense that your parent *has* to do this or that?

If you're really struggling with this and feel stuck in a rut of conflict and frustration, getting input from a professional counselor (together or on your own) can help.

What This Looks Like: The Smiths and The Johnsons

Example 1: The Smiths

Capacity and communication: these two common snags were clearly tripping up the Smith siblings in their efforts to help their father, Albert.

While Albert was able to manage his self-care (meals, dressing, bathing), was he capable of continuing to manage his finances? While he was functionally able to drive, did he have the capacity to appreciate whether he was still able to do so safely?

First, Zeke and his siblings considered Albert's capacity in light of a few specific situations. Did he seem to have capacity to understand his medical issues and bring them up to his doctor? He seemed too forgetful. Did he have capacity to manage the finances safely? The huge checks to his neighbors and missed bills suggested no. Did he have capacity to determine whether he should keep driving? He seemed unaware of his tickets and fender benders. In short, his mental capacities for several domains seemed questionable.

Given these capacity issues, Zeke decides that it seems ethically permissible to try contacting his father's doctor, even though Albert insists he's fine.

Zeke also recalls that the POAs are springing, which means he'll need to get Albert's capacity issues documented in order for him to be able to act.

Finally, Zeke and his siblings review how they've been communicating with Albert and reflect on that. They realize they've been trying to get Albert to "see" and "understand" what he's having trouble with but that hasn't seemed to lead Albert to any insights or agreements. They decide to abandon their efforts to convince him of danger and worry and instead now focus on helping Albert feel heard and validated during upcoming conversations.

Example 2: The Johnsons

Thinking about the situation in terms of her mother's capacity and her own communication style is new for Sue.

As she learns about capacity and thinks about her mom's frequent forgetfulness and confusion, she thinks perhaps her mom doesn't quite have capacity to make an informed decision to forgo medical evaluation of her problems. This realization helps Sue feel a little better about trying to push for a medical evaluation over her mother's wishes.

Next, Sue thinks about her mother's POA situation. Maria is forgetful but she's amenable to Sue's help and generally trusts Sue. Sue hopes that an attorney would agree that her mother might have capacity to sign a POA for healthcare and also for general affairs.

Reflecting on communication, Sue realizes that she's been arguing with her aunt about her mom's condition and this isn't productive. She knows she'll need her as an ally if there are difficulties ahead and resolves to take steps to avoid arguments and solicit her opinion so she feels included.

Sue also realizes that because her mom is a lifelong doctor avoider, continuing to argue with her about seeing someone is stressful and counterproductive to their relationship. She decides to continue exploring ways to get Maria more help that doesn't feel like pressure, using more empathy and positives when the subject comes up. For the first time, Sue also considers that she may also just have to accept that her mom might get less medical care overall than Sue would prefer for her.

PART THREE: TAKING ACTION

PUTTING TOGETHER WHAT YOU'VE LEARNED, TO PLAN AND ATTEMPT A NEXT STEP FORWARD—AND WHAT TO DO WHEN SNAGS HAPPEN (THEY PROBABLY WILL)

Now what? Hopefully having a better sense of what an ideal approach would look like, along with insights into the two biggest snags, gives you a better sense of direction. Now it's time to plan and execute your help for your aging parent.

Here's the thing, though: we'd love to be able to tell you exactly what to do next and how to do it so that it will work on the first try.

But helping older parents doesn't work that way.

First of all, no book can tell you just what to do in your personal situation, with *your* parent. Chapter 5 gives you lots of suggestions to help you form your own plan. In general, though, the next steps you pick will be based on the particulars of what's going on with your parent and your family. (If you want case-specific direction on exactly what to do next, you'll have to consider hiring a professional, like a geriatric care manager, who can work closely with you and your family to make it happen.)

Next, and even more important for you to know: **whatever you do next probably won't work on the first try.**

Ever hear the expression, "No plan survives contact with reality"? (It comes from the military saying, "No battle plan survives contact with the enemy.")

The saying reflects the truism that things almost never work out according to the original plan because it's impossible to predict just how other parties involved will react.

So instead, the savvy person makes a plan AND expects that they'll have to adjust the plan as they go along, based on what happens in real time.

Especially when it comes to older adults, it's sensible to assume that you'll have to try a few times when attempting whatever next step you've decided to focus on. In between attempts, it's incredibly useful to engage in a little reflecting and adjusting. We like to refer to this as "experimenting."

In our experience, 99 percent of the time when helping aging adults, it takes some iterating on the part of families (and of involved professionals) before noticeable progress happens. We also believe it's necessary to iterate a given approach at least a few times before concluding that "it's not working" and deciding it's time to try something quite different.

If you go into your next steps expecting to have to experiment, you'll be less likely to be disappointed and deeply frustrated when things don't quite work out the very first time.

To recap, here's our recommended approach for taking thoughtful, informed action to help an aging parent:

- Decide what your next step to try will be.

- Try it, experiment, and adjust as needed.

Chapter 5 will give you a little more guidance on taking those next steps.

And then in Chapter 6, we'll offer suggestions on handling some of the most common obstacles families encounter as they do this.

Chapter 5:
Plan Your Next Step(s),
and Try Them

It's huge progress to have a clearer sense of what might best improve your parent's situation, as the previous chapters have hopefully given you.

Now it's time to actually decide on what you're going to attempt and give it a try.

If you're like most families, when you reviewed what's going on with your parents (Chapters 1 and 2), you uncovered a long list of issues.

And then in Chapter 3, in which we explain the common "ideal" next steps, you probably saw that there were several next steps that would be optimal to tackle first.

People can easily get overwhelmed at this point. So much going on, so much that "should" be done.

It's normal to feel lost or frozen. But you don't want to stay there; it's not constructive. Here's a practical way forward.

Deciding on Your Next Step(s): Think A-B-C-D-E

This simple process can be applied in any situation to help you help an older adult. An overview:

A. ASSESS: First, you want to recap the assessment you've made of the situation so far—those key things that are an issue for your aging parent (what you know so far) and your parent's/family's priorities.

B. BRAINSTORM: You'll then weigh your options, considering:

- What seems most urgent/important to address?

- What seems most feasible? (Compare the pros and cons.)

C. CHOOSE AND PLAN: Based on what you brainstormed, pick the one to three issues you're going to focus on tackling next, and then for each one, plan some specific next steps.

D. DO: Give it your best go, taking the next steps you've planned using your best communication skills and considering capacity issues, if appropriate (which it often is).

E. EXPERIMENT: Based on how things go, you'll reassess, adjust your approach, and likely try again. (This is also known as iterating.)

Let's break out each part into more detail.

DOWNLOADABLE CHEATSHEET: THE A-B-C WAY: A PROCESS FOR PICKING YOUR NEXT STEPS, AND TRYING THEM

You can use this worksheet, which summarizes the process, to help you keep your thoughts organized as you go along. (See RESOURCES.)

A. ASSESS: What's your sense of the key issues and facts here?

It helps to write this down in list form. Refer to your notes or lists you made using the tools in Chapter 1, as well as the "ideal" next steps described in Chapter 3. Be sure to consider:

- Does it seem like there's a significant memory or thinking issue (a.k.a. "cognitive impairment") going on?

- Main life task issues you think your parent needs help with (Function).

- Key safety issues (Safety).

- What's known so far about health conditions and any past evaluation (Causes).

- Does your parent need a current medical evaluation?

- If your parent has had a recent evaluation, do you know the results?

- Legal documents and who is named.

- Do you (or someone else in family) have authority to get health info?

- Do you (or someone else in family) have authority to help with business or financial affairs?

- Do you think your parent's mental capacities are impaired?

- Is your parent open to your involvement and help, or resistant, or somewhere in between?

ALSO ASSESS: HOW DOES YOUR PARENT SEEM TO SEE THE SITUATION?

The second part of your review should consider how the key players are feeling about what's going on. You can also jot this down (or refer to notes made in Chapter 2). Be sure to think about:

- What's your parent's take on the issues you're concerned about? Have they voiced any specific concerns, complaints, worries, or problems?

- How are their perceptions similar to, or different from, yours?

- What's their vision of how you could or should be helping?

- Do they seem open to outside help?

- Have they said or signaled what's most important to them (either in a recent conversation or in the past)? In other words, do you have a sense of their goals and priorities? Their fears or concerns?

Last but not least: what do other family players think?

As you do this, review which ways of communicating with your parent and others have worked okay in the past. Anything that hasn't worked?

B. BRAINSTORM: List the issues you might help with and what's involved

Based on your thinking above, come up with a list of the issues you want to attempt to address in order to help your parent and what that might involve.

At this point, just jot down all the likely options that come to mind.

Then list pros and cons of addressing each item. Consider how high the stakes are (to health, safety, relationship), and how feasible accomplishing something seems, to help you identify where to start. You'll want to especially focus on:

- How could you take a next step towards getting a medical evaluation and/or diagnosis (if needed)?

- How could you take a next step towards addressing function or safety issues?

- Who could help you? Should you consider bringing in another family member or even a professional? (Consider people who might help you to brainstorm, if you feel stuck or if you feel like others should have a voice in this, as well as who could advise you or help you carry out a plan.)

It can help to review Chapter 3 to see the *ideal* next steps for most situations.

C. CHOOSE AND PLAN: Choose one to three things from your list and plan your action steps

Review the results of your brainstorming sessions. You might have a short list or a long one. Now you want to choose what you're going to try to take action on.

Don't get too hung up on making the "right" or "best" choice. Trust that if you've gone through the steps above, you'll be making a reasonable choice. That's good enough.

In general, we recommend choosing between one and three items to try to take action on for starters; attempting to plan, execute, and iterate more than three different issues is likely to be overwhelming.

TO HELP YOU CHOOSE:

What if there are multiple things to do on your list after brainstorming and you're having trouble deciding which to tackle first? Here are some strategies to break it down and decide where to focus:

- Address the "red flag" concerns—immediate threats to safety—first.

- Factor in feasibility. Which things can you knock off most easily? Sometimes addressing relatively small things your parent is in agreement with, or that you can manage without a lot of resistance, can marginally improve the situation (and smooth cooperation overall) so you're then in a better position to tackle something more complicated.

- See if you can address what's especially important to your parent early on. Even if it's not the real crux of the problem, you can earn goodwill and cooperation about other ideas by showing that you're listening.

- Otherwise, decide which item, or few items, feels most important to you in terms of addressing key aspects of the ideal plan. This answer looks different for everyone because there are so many variables in each situation. For many families, following up on the medical evaluation and addressing function and safety issues will be high on the list.

- If there are other decisionmakers or helpers you can consult, be sure to do so. Find out what they perceive as the priorities and their individual strengths. Remember, stakeholders in a situation (your other parent or your parent's partner, siblings) usually like to be involved, especially if only part of the burden falls on their shoulders rather than the whole thing. Try to divide-and-conquer based on others' skill sets and interests.

TO HELP YOU PLAN AND MAKE YOUR PRIORITIES ACTIONABLE:

Each issue you've identified is probably a relatively big thing. To tackle it, you'll want to break things down into a few concrete "sub-steps"—almost like a specific To-Do list. Usually these sub-steps fall into these categories:

- Something to research (a health problem, a legal point, a service, an agency, experts, and so on).

- Something to do (make a call or appointment, tour a facility, review medication, hire someone, and so on).

- A conversation to have with your parent (or sometimes someone else, like a consultant, the doctor, a neutral third party, a sibling, your other parent, and so on).

This is a good time to ask others for a little advice. Consider asking friends or colleagues who've been in the same boat, or online groups, or others you can think of questions like: How did you try doing this? What happened? What do you wish you'd known? Do you have recommendations for [an eldercare manager, a home care agency, etc.]? Do you know anyone good at [a particular medical center, an agency, etc.]?

D. DO: Attempt your next step(s)

Now that you've chosen what issue(s) you're going to address and planned some specific ways to make it happen, it's time to execute your intervention.

Remember: Think about how to bring your best communication skills. You can't control whether your parent (or the system) will cooperate but you can control your part of the conversation.

And again: Expect things not to go smoothly. After all, no plan entirely survives contact with reality.

E. EXPERIMENT: Reassess how things went and (likely) try again

It would be nice if checking everything off your To-Do list resulted, magically, in Problem Solved. In the real world, of course, obstacles abound.

You'll often have to bring something up or attempt an improvement a few times to make headway.

For example, maybe you'll need to have a certain conversation multiple times with your parent, as you find the best time to talk or experiment with different phrasings to help them get used to an idea. Maybe you try one kind of service, then later find out about something else that might work better. Or you hire a personal-care aide who clashes with your parent's personality and needs to be replaced.

These are iterations: different ways of attempting a particular intervention or tweaking the way you tackle an issue.

Eventually, you may reach a point where an altogether different approach to helping your parent may be in order. That's a little different and we'll cover those kinds of crossroads in Part Four.

At this point, expect that you may need to come at a particular issue several different ways. In other words, "try and try again."

WHAT HELPS AS YOU CYCLE THROUGH DOING AND EXPERIMENTING:

- *Try keeping a written log of what you've done* (made a call, had a conversation, put a given support in place) and when. You might think you'll remember everything but details, dates, and even reactions tend to run together over time. It's also a good way to organize contact information and helps keep things transparent, if other family members want to know what's going on.

- *Just expect to go slowly and take the long view of things.* It would be great if you could achieve everything you want to overnight. That's probably not realistic. Your parent may need time to process and come around to certain changes. Or dealing with the medical system can take more time than you might like to get appointments, records, or even phone calls returned. With more of a "macro" view of progress, you're more likely to be patient, rather than frustrated. You'll be less likely to beat yourself up for not "solving" everything right away.

- *When you feel especially stuck, go over the communication tips in Chapters 1 and 4.* Surprisingly often, a lot of progress can be power-packed within the approach you use, especially with your parent but also with other family members. Backing off and then trying again later, with a slightly different approach or different language, can sometimes yield greater acceptance.

- *Be aware that certain obstacles tend to require lots of iterating.* We cover these in Chapter 6. Again, it's to be expected.

Last but not least:

REMEMBER THERE ARE NO SIMPLE SOLUTIONS (SORRY!) AND IT'S NORMAL FOR THIS TO BE HARD

Helping an older parent can take so many forms. There's no single "right" way to do it. There's not even a "best" way that any doctor or other professional can point you to.

There are only possibilities. And moving toward any of them counts as potential progress.

Of course, this also means the process is rarely easy. It's normal, in fact, for this to be very hard!

That's important to keep in mind as you go. Don't beat yourself up over how slowly things may seem to go or how much resistance you encounter. Keep trying.

Certain "roadblocks" are especially common. Chapter 6, "Workarounds for Common Obstacles," offers extra advice for moving through them. (And if at the end of that you still find yourself at a long-term impasse, there's more in Chapter 7, "If at First You Don't Succeed...")

What This Looks Like: The Smiths and The Johnsons

Example 1: The Smiths

When the Smith siblings go through the process described in this chapter, here's what it looks like:

A. Assess: The adult children (who live in different places) organize a group video chat and start off by recapping the key issues and facts they've assessed so far:

- Their father's memory and thinking definitely seems worse than it used to be. The siblings are pretty sure this has been going on for months, but they have no idea whether Albert's doctor is aware and whether Albert has had any cognitive evaluation

- He seems to be having trouble paying bills on time. He is having fender benders and is getting traffic tickets, and they've observed careless driving when with him in the car. Otherwise, he seems to be managing his key life tasks okay for now.

- The key safety issues right now seem to be:

  - Driving: seems risky, he could get hurt or potentially hurt someone else.

  - Finances: If he's missing bill payments, could that have significant consequences beyond late fees? Plus, his large checks to neighbors leave the siblings feeling he could easily be scammed or otherwise mismanage his finances.

- Regarding mental capacities: The siblings are concerned about Albert's memory problems and poor awareness of what's been going on. They wonder whether he might be developing Alzheimer's or another form of dementia. They agree he might currently lack the capacity to truly understand certain decisions or manage certain things, such as his finances. But as far as they know, no expert has weighed in on Albert's capacities.

- Zeke is named in DPOA documents but these are springing. He reviews the criteria for Albert being incapacitated and it says, *"I am incapacitated whenever my regular attending physician provides a written opinion that I am unable to effectively manage my property or financial affairs, or if two licensed physicians provide an opinion to this effect."* So for Zeke to be able to act as agent, they'll need Albert's doctor—or two other doctors—to confirm that Albert has lost capacity.

- The siblings reflect on their understanding of how Albert sees all this, along with his goals and priorities:

  - He's been resistant to help.

  - He either can't see the problems around him or is refusing to admit it (they aren't sure which).

- He wants to keep living as he's doing, and it's really important to him to remain independent.

B. Brainstorm: The Smith siblings then brainstorm options for what their next attempts to help Albert might look like:

- Contact Albert's primary care provider to see if Albert's been evaluated and also if the doctor agrees Albert's capacity is slipping. (PROS: This seems really important. CONS: How to do it?)

- See if the doctor is willing to advise Albert to not drive. (PROS: The doctor becomes the "bad guy." CONS: Albert will be furious and then needs a way to get around.)

- Look into reporting Albert to the DMV. (PROS: It might keep him safe. CONS: If he finds out, he'll be furious.)

- Get help determining how to "activate" the POA. They are pretty sure Albert's doctor would have to provide an opinion but they wonder if there's more they should know about this. (PROS: This may be needed going forward. CONS: Again, it means starting with the doctor.)

  - They consider whether to consult with a professional, such an attorney or geriatric care manager. (PROS: A third-party expert sounds useful since they live far away. CONS: They don't really see any downside other than the cost involved.)

- Finances:

  - Talk to Albert about letting one of them assist with finances. (PROS: It's a safeguard. CONS: Albert is likely to resist.)

- Look into automatic billpaying services. (PROS: They can do this even before engaging Albert. CONS: They still need his input to make it happen.)

- Review Albert's meds next time they're there to see if any of them might be making him worse. (PROS: This seems an easy safeguard. CONS: They can't think of any.)

C. Choose: The siblings look over their list. It all sounds worth doing but they know they need to pick just one to three for now.

After discussion, they decide it would be especially valuable to reach out to Albert's doctor, to make sure he's aware of Albert's difficulties with driving and finances, and to find out how he might be able to help Albert and their family.

They also decide to look for a geriatric care manager based in Albert's city to advise them regarding next steps and because a friend pointed out that it can be very helpful to have someone there "on the ground."

After this lengthy conversation, the siblings agree to take a break and convene again a few days later.

Zeke and his siblings spend their next virtual meeting strategizing about how to connect with Albert's doctor. Albert hasn't been very forthcoming in the past about what his doctor says, although they aren't sure whether that's because their father doesn't remember versus not wanting to share. They decide to see if Zeke might be able to accompany him to an appointment. They know that Albert usually has a calendar at home and that he puts appointments on it. At his next weekend visit to his father, Zeke takes a look and makes note of the date and time of the upcoming appointment—it's in three weeks.

He then arranges to be visiting Albert during that time. He's planning to offer to come along for the visit. He'll tell Albert that since he's impressed with how well Albert is doing, he'd love to come along and say hi to the doctor, whom he's known over the years, and tell him so and treat Albert to lunch after.

Meanwhile, the siblings will draft a letter to the doctor outlining their concerns, which they'll send before the appointment. (Remember, under HIPAA rules, it's fine to convey information *to* healthcare providers about another person even if the provider can't or won't disclose that patient's health information to you.)

Lastly, they plan to look for a local geriatric care manager.

D. Do: Zeke sends the siblings' summary of concerns to Albert's doctor. He tells his father he plans to visit.

Meanwhile, Zeke's sister starts to research geriatric care managers in Albert's city. She starts by using the online tool at the Aging Life Care Professionals website to locate some possibilities. Then she calls a friend who is a nurse nearby to see if she has any suggestions. Next, she plans to call a few of the candidates to learn more.

E. Experiment: The first geriatric care manager candidate, recommended by Zeke's sister's friend (a nurse), is not taking on new clients. But the woman offers to ask around for other suggestions. So Zeke's sister keeps trying.

Zeke, on the other hand, is less successful in his plan to find out whether his dad has had his cognitive symptoms adequately evaluated. Although Albert allowed him to join him at the appointment (eager to show off his good health to his son, and his son to his doctor, and to have lunch after), the doctor simply did a cursory check of how he was managing his current meds. He didn't address any cognitive problems. When Zeke persisted, hoping to drop hints that alluded to the letter he'd sent ("Isn't there some kind of screening recommended for patients Albert's age?"), the doctor brushed it off. "He's in great shape for his age. He's just getting older—we all are!"

This didn't seem satisfactory to Zeke because he again had witnessed the erratic driving and a fair amount of repetition. Nor did he have a clear understanding of whether there had been any kind of recent cognitive evaluation in the past—neither the doctor nor Albert were forthcoming about this. Yet he dreaded hurting his father's pride and adding stress to their relationship by saying something in front of him. Zeke realizes he'll have to approach the issue another way and feels that activating the POA is more urgent than ever. (We provide ideas he can apply to this obstacle in Chapter 6.)

Example 2: The Johnsons

When Sue Johnson thinks through her situation and uses the A-B-C-D-E formula, it looks like this:

A. Assess: She and her mother, Maria, are both concerned about Maria's memory and thinking skills, although Sue is more eager to get a medical opinion about what's going on and whether Maria might be clinically depressed. She's unsure how much to worry about possible safety issues, like using the stove or tripping and falling on the growing clutter. Maria seems open to help but Sue isn't certain what kind she most needs and would most accept. More help around the house? Help managing money? Companionship for her obvious loneliness since her husband's death?

B. Brainstorm: Sue makes a list of options and considers their benefits and difficulties and how feasible each item is:

- Get her mother to a doctor for a medical evaluation. (PROS: May get clarity about what's going on cognitively and will at least get Maria connected with someone who can help with health needs going forward. CONS: Maria is very resistant to seeing a doctor.)

- Get legal documents prepared. (PROS: These documents sound useful to Sue and she thinks her mother is cognitively "with it" enough to get them drawn up. CONS: Sue isn't sure where to begin.)

- Research other ways to get healthy meals delivered. (PROS: This could be a timesaver. CONS: Will it cost money? Will Maria like the idea?)

- Figure out how to get more time to help her shop, clean, and manage money. (PROS: This, too, can spare Sue time. CONS: She feels like she doesn't have the time to think about it!)

- Implement other ways to keep her mom safe in the house (stove guards, clean up clutter). (PROS: Maria will be less likely to fall or hurt herself. CONS: Sue can't think of any, other than the time involved.)

- Look into senior programs or hiring an elder companion to provide more social outlets. (PROS: Social stimulation might really help Maria overall. CONS: Sue can't think of any, other than the best way to make it happen.)

C. Choose: The most urgent thing seems to get Maria to a doctor for a cognitive evaluation and to check for clinical depression. Because she hasn't had any medical care recently and is showing concerning signs, this seems to be the absolute best starting place, Sue decides. She really wants her mom to get plugged into the medical community. It occurs to her that her own doctor's practice might be a natural place to start.

The other big thing she decides it's a good time to work on is persuading her mother to get a POA for finances and healthcare.

Meanwhile, she'll continue the small steps she's been doing, like providing meals and taking her mom shopping, until she can figure out better solutions. She's wary of tackling too much all at once. She resolves to also try engaging her aunt in ways that are more supportive and less contentious, since she's a natural choice to provide her sister with more socializing and is able to help her everyday functioning in other ways.

D. Do: First Sue asks Maria if she's okay with her making an appointment with Sue's own doctor: "Look, we're both worried about your memory, and you haven't seen a doctor in years." Maria says no way. "I'm fine." Sue isn't surprised but she's disappointed, considering how open her mother has been to her help in other ways. In the past, Sue would have tried to convince Maria of the wisdom in getting a checkup and told her she was being irresponsible by not seeing a doctor. This time, she stopped herself when she saw the suggestion was not well received. Instead, she let it ride a bit.

Several days later, when Maria is in a good mood, Sue mentions that she heard that National Healthcare Decisions Day is coming up. "They said on the news that everyone over 55 is supposed to have documents in place for future financial and healthcare decision-making. I never heard that before but it makes sense. It seems like 'life housekeeping' and you know how much I like being organized! Hey, let's try it together. It'll give us something to do this weekend." This approach normalizes the idea of POAs rather than framing the issue as "You're doing poorly and I'm going to need a POA!"

In the meantime, she continues helping her mom with shopping, cooking, and cleaning as best she can. But because she's now doing these things while thinking in the back of her mind how to get help with them, they seem slightly less hassle to her.

She's also reached out to her aunt in a neutral, non-argumentative way. Instead of complaining about Maria's condition, she's emphasized to her aunt that her mom sounds like she needs to do something fun and have some company, and could she help her with that?

E. Experiment: Sue has success with everything except the medical appointment. Because her mother is completely resistant to the idea, she decides to wait a week before bringing it up again. This is a common obstacle. When she tries again, she'll use some of the approaches we describe in the next chapter.

Maria is fine with preparing the POAs along with her daughter, since it's been framed as an activity for both of them, rather than an issue directly concerning her own condition. And the aunt accepts the suggestion to do something social with her sister, Maria. She invites her to go shopping and have lunch at a favorite restaurant. Unfortunately, this proves to be a bit too much activity for Maria, who seems tired and overwhelmed and asks to cut the outing short. What's more, Sue's aunt—who still believes the issue is grieving rather than cognitive trouble—doesn't seem to take the hint to make it a regular outing. Sue sees she'll need to continue looking for other ways to give her mom helpful social stimulation.

Chapter 6:
Use These Workarounds
for Common Obstacles

As you attempt to help your aging parent, you can pretty much count on the need to iterate—continuing to thoughtfully tweak your efforts to figure out what works. Despite your best A-B-C-D-E efforts, you might still feel stuck.

This chapter presents some of the most common situations that can block progress and, for each, suggests how you might find another way.

There's no "right" or "wrong" or single approach to any given issue. Whatever your specific goal (getting a dangerous driver off the road, preventing more falls, safeguarding finances, exploring a move), these are ways to break through stalemates and daunting roadblocks.

A few things can help as you go:

- **Keep a written log of your efforts.** Note what you tried, how it was received, and why it did or didn't work. Include any relevant contacts you made (along with phone numbers or other contact info so everything is all in one place). You might think you'll remember everything but as time goes on, dates, places, and people can run together. Having notes to refer to will help as you reassess what's been tried and plan later attempts.

- **Give some good thought to what might be at the heart of a given obstacle.** Sometimes it's not what's on the surface but something a little deeper. Look for patterns. Listen for the emotions behind what people are saying.

- **Reflect on how your efforts at good communication and connection are going.** We know, you've probably already tried to be thoughtful about how you're communicating with your parent. We also know that the less progress you're making, the easier it is to grow frustrated or impatient. But especially when you're facing obstacles, it's important to keep reflecting on how that's going and how you can keep trying to make it a little better.

- **Get others' input on what to try.** For ideas, you might:

  - Check in with other family members. Asking others for their ideas or reactions can also be a useful way to get them involved in the situation and feel invested in helping to resolve it. That's why you want to both brainstorm with them at the outset and then keep them in the loop as you move forward, whether there's success or not.

  - Post questions to caregivers in online forums. You're bound to get a variety of suggestions from those in similar situations or who have overcome the same sort of obstacle. There's a lot of clever thinking and generosity of spirit out there!

  - Consult with a relevant professional. Most people don't need to hire an expert for every issue. But in some cases, it can save you time, headaches, and even money to involve someone with direct expertise on elder law, housing, occupational therapy (for things like driving evaluations), geriatric care or medicine, or another area you know little about.

Now here are suggestions for specific challenges:

If Your Parent Won't Get Checked

As we've seen, a medical evaluation when there are cognitive symptoms is an important starting point—but it's only useful IF your parent will go. How can you overcome resistance or denial and get a reluctant person to have a cognitive evaluation?

Try This:

- **Frame the checkup as a way for you to help your parent with his or her goals.** "Since you want to [stay in this house, take a big trip, keep driving], why not check with the doctor to make sure you've got everything covered to stay strong and healthy enough for that." Or "I know you're very healthy, but I read a report recently on how it's fairly common for older adults to experience [car accidents, falls, mistakes] that are being caused by very treatable health issues such as the blood chemistry being a little off or medication side effects. I've asked my doctor to check me for those; let's ask your doctor so we can be sure your independence isn't affected by one of these."

- **Avoid calling it a "dementia evaluation."** Likewise, avoid emphasizing that the purpose is to check out memory concerns. That's usually alarming to people. Unless your parent has expressly framed their concern this way, it's probably better to refer to general health or empathize and emphasize positive outcomes: "Whatever we find out, nothing will change overnight. You'll still be the same person who walked into the doctor's office. But you'll know better what's going on and can do something about it." (It's true there's no cure yet for Alzheimer's, but there are many ways to mitigate symptoms, plan for a good future, and even slow disease progress. And remember, many cognitive symptoms reveal non-dementia health issues.)

- **Peg a checkup on some preexisting reason to see the doctor.** For example, you might piggyback a cognitive evaluation on an appointment for such reasons as to follow up for another condition, to refill an expiring medication, a fall that warrants checking out, time for an annual flu shot or shingles vaccine, or the DMV requiring an exam for license renewal (this requirement varies by state). Or use another possible motivation your parent might have for seeing the doctor as a pretext to get him or her in: to have another symptom (fatigue, arthritis, headaches, a skin condition) looked at, for example, or to get medical clearance before a trip or a new exercise program.

- **Try asking as a favor to you.** "I'll feel so much better if we just make sure all your records and medications are up-to-date. I know you think I always overdo it with the recordkeeping, so I appreciate you're helping me feel more peace of mind."

- **Enlist your parent's doctor to be an ally**. This can be a good option if your parent has a well-established relationship with a doctor they respect. If the doctor is willing to recommend that your parent come in, that can carry a lot of weight with some older adults.

- **Enlist your other parent (or parent's partner) or another trusted source to be an ally** who can encourage your parent. It might work if the partner suggests they both get general checkups, even if the concern is just about the one with memory issues.

- **Consider the "fiblet."** We know caregivers who have said that THEY need an appointment and want their parent to accompany them into the exam room. (In this case, the doctor was notified in advance that the exam was really about the parent and addressed both "patients.") Or invent a plausible reason: "The insurance company needs you to get a physical." Remember, if it seems like your parent's mental capacities may be slipping, then it's often ethically permissible to fudge the truth or even tell a small fib, if that's what it takes to get them something that truly is important for their health, safety, or well-being.

- **Tread lightly in the face of dug-in resistance.** While you're smart to stick to your resolve about having concerns checked out, realize that sometimes you need to slow down. If you badger or bicker about it, you risk setting up a power struggle. Maybe drop the subject for a few weeks before returning with a new approach.

Meanwhile, continue to document a record of behaviors and issues you find concerning—then try again or try one of the following three suggestions.

1. **Send written word to your parent's primary care provider about your concerns.** It's best to summarize your most important observations and concerns on a single page (you can provide more details in additional pages if you want but those may or may not get read). Be sure to include a specific "ask," spelling out what you're hoping the provider will do for your parent or your family. Follow up with a phone call to make sure that it arrived and your request is clear. The provider may be able to convince your parent to come in for a check. If you specifically ask for their discretion, the information you provide may be held in confidence so your parent doesn't have to know it came from you. (For more on this, see the following Roadblock section.)

2. **Recruit a provider to come to the home.** Although not available everywhere, some doctors and health providers do make house calls. This might be a service that you need to pay for out of pocket, although occasionally you'll find a provider available who will accept your parent's insurance.

3. **Consider engaging a geriatric care manager (GCM, or aging life care professional).** Consultants on managing all aspects of aging care, these professionals are skilled at working with older adults and might be able to persuade a wary or resistant parent to get checked. They,

too, make house calls. To get in the door for an initial home visit, the GCM might suggest creative solutions, like using the guise of something that seems unrelated to a memory/cognition or health check, like home organizing or to talk through a move under consideration. You could even consider introducing the GCM as a local researcher who is interviewing older adults for a local history project or to study "healthy aging." Again, think about how you can frame introducing the GCM as something that will appeal to your parent.

If Your Parent Doesn't Want You Present at a Checkup...or Isn't Comfortable With You Talking About Them There... (or You're Not Comfortable Yourself)

Many people who may be willing enough to have concerning symptoms checked out nevertheless don't want their adult children present. In other situations, the patient is fine having an adult child in the room, but one or the other of you is uncomfortable about being frank with the doctor about what's going on. Don't feel bad; this is very common. These conversations can feel awkward.

In any of these cases, an effective workaround is to send a short summary of your concerns to the doctor before the appointment. There's no legal restriction against you doing this, and for the provider, it's useful to know in advance the actual purpose of the visit. It helps us zero in on cognitive status and possible causes more quickly and with the right tact.

Here's how to do this in a way that gets the job done—while feeling better about it.

Try This:

- First, consider *avoiding* asking your parent's permission to

furnish this information: Ideally, of course, you'd respectfully ask if your parent minded your speaking up with the provider and they'd say, "Sure." In the real world, some people will give their consent if explicitly asked but those who are already defensive or resistant, or who are intensely private, will say NO (or refuse to come to the visit at all). That friction can make it even harder for you to then take the step of going behind their back to share concerns with a provider, even if you strongly feel it's necessary.

It can be better not to ask in the first place.

Instead: Get comfortable with the idea of working around your parent to tip off the doctor about cognitive concerns without asking explicit permission first. We don't mean to sound cavalier about this—this can be a fraught choice. But it can also be a good way to get the ball rolling.

You may have heard about "HIPAA" (Health Insurance Portability and Accountability Act) rules and worry they bar you from communicating with the doctor. The part of the act people are typically referring to in these circumstances is a federal privacy rule mandated by HIPPA that governs how health providers must protect the privacy of an individual's medical information. The HIPAA Privacy Rule affects "covered entities:" health providers, health insurers, and other kinds of professionals who handle medical information. Families and other private citizens aren't covered by this rule. This means that you aren't obligated to maintain your parent's confidentiality about medical information the way providers are.

You don't need legal permission to disclose or convey information to someone else's physician. Doing so is more of a relationship quandary.

- **To help you feel less paralyzed (or less bad) about making the decision to share your concerns with the doctor:**

Weigh the pros and cons of sharing this information. On the

plus side, you'll be fast-tracking your parent's ability to get accurate help. Or you may decide things aren't really so bad and you'll wait and see a bit longer. On the negative side, your relationship might suffer if your parent found out. Or you may decide it's worth the short-term bump for which you can ask for forgiveness later. Or you may forever conceal that you took this step and they never find out.

Imagine how your parent might feel about the doctor knowing this information. Sometimes we assume things that aren't necessarily true. Has your parent said things in the past that suggest he or she would want the best medical treatment? Thinking about it from this perspective can help you become more comfortable with the decision.

Check who's legally authorized to make medical decisions for your parent. There may not be anyone else but in some cases there's a durable power of attorney in place that names you or another relative (a spouse, another child) you can enlist to help. We've seen cases where someone was named in paperwork drawn up years earlier then forgotten.

- **If you decide to send a written preview to the doctor before your parent's appointment—a recommended step—follow these tips to make your message useful:**

Keep it short so it fits on one page. If it's too long, the doctor is less likely to review and/or absorb it all.

Summarize the most important relevant things at the top, almost like an executive summary.

Specify your concerns: what sorts of changes you're seeing, for how long, and how they're interfering with everyday life.

Be explicit in the summary how your parent feels about your involvement, as a heads-up to the doctor. For example, "I think my father would be upset if I bring up these concerns, so I'd appreciate your discretion." Or "My mom gets defensive about her memory; please hold in confidence that this information is coming from me." This allows the professional to plan accordingly what to cover and how to say it discreetly. (For example, Dr. K might say to such a patient, "I have all my patients take this quick test…")

See a sample letter, below.

Follow up your written message with a phone call before the appointment. Check in with the front office to be sure the doctor got your summary and has seen it.

Pro tip: Bring an additional copy to the medical visit and pass it to the medical assistant, along with a note saying you just want to make sure the doctor is aware of this info. You can also ask at this time if the doctor can please allow you to talk to him or her for a minute or two before or after the visit.

- **Know that when you're in the room with your parent, a verbal okay is sufficient under HIPAA rules for the health provider to talk about the patient's condition.** If your parent doesn't mind your being there and hearing firsthand what the doctor has to say, that's ideal. You don't have to stop and sign any special paperwork.

TOOL: SAMPLE DOCTOR LETTER

You can use this sample letter, written by Zeke Smith from the "What This Looks Like" family stories, as a guide for how you might share concerns with your parent's provider:

Dear Dr. Adams:

I'm the son of your patient, Albert Smith. He has an appointment with you at 9:00 a.m. on Wednesday, May 5.

I'm writing to let you know of some memory and thinking problems my brother and sister and I have been noticing in our father over these past several months. He denies any problems when we try to talk to him about it and, therefore, I doubt he'll bring these up to you.

Since this seems to be an important health issue, however, we want to make sure you're aware so that you can take appropriate action to evaluate him medically.

Here are the specific things we have noticed:

- He's had four small traffic accidents in 18 months and received two traffic tickets, which he forgot to pay.

- While driving with him, I've observed him run through a stop sign, drive well below the speed limit, and almost hit a pedestrian he didn't see; he also has trouble turning to look over his shoulder.

- He's missed multiple bill payments over the past year, which is unlike him; he's also written several large unnecessary checks to neighbors.

- He's increasingly forgetful about appointments and repeats himself often in conversations, which is a change from a year or two ago.

Because of these changes, we're worried that he's developing memory problems and are wondering if this might be something like Alzheimer's?

We are also worried about his safety, when it comes to driving and also managing his finances. We're hoping you'll be able to advise him and us as to how to address the issues and keep him safe.

Because he became upset with us when we mentioned his doctor should know about these changes, we would appreciate your discretion in not revealing that we have tipped you off. We are having difficulty getting him to let us help him, and we're worried about him becoming angry with us if he finds out about this letter.

Thank you,
Zeke Smith
202-555-5555

If The Medical Exam Doesn't Seem Useful

What if your parent has had a medical evaluation but you're not satisfied with what was done about cognitive symptoms or with the doctor's conclusions? Perhaps, the doctor just asked a few cursory questions before saying she sees nothing in particular to worry about or observes that your parent is just "getting old," when you're convinced there have been worrisome changes.

This is difficult but unfortunately rather common. We recommend diplomatically trying to engage in conversation, both to better understand the doctor's thinking and to persuade him or her to do more. If that doesn't work—or if you've already concluded the doctor's not receptive or able to do more—you'll have to consider getting a second opinion.

Here are some specific approaches:

Try This:

- **Don't be afraid to speak up.** Persist with the doctor in bringing up the issues you've observed, asking him or her to clarify what they think is causing this. Try phrases like, "Help me to understand what you think is causing Mom's [paranoia, falls, forgetfulness]." Or "Please help me to understand why you think this isn't a worrisome problem that requires more evaluation." Or try rephrasing their words to be sure you understand correctly: "So you're saying that...is that right?"

- **Be polite but informed—and ask for their help**. If they didn't seem to check all the items that are part of a cognitive evaluation, bring in your worksheet and specifically ask for help in addressing the items. It's important to be as diplomatic as possible. It often helps to specify that you value their professional expertise and their help, and since you know the practice is busy, you've brought a guide so you can efficiently ask about a few more things to make sure your parent has had a thorough evaluation. Invite them to go over it with you.

- **Try framing any capacity questions as specifically as you can.** Doctors can be reluctant to label someone as globally incapacitated unless there's very obvious advanced dementia. But if you ask for their opinion regarding specific activities, they can often be more helpful. (Remember: When someone asks a doctor if a patient is competent or has capacity, the doctor's response should be, "For what?" because capacity assessments are supposed to be situation-specific, as we explained in Chapter 4. But be forewarned: They may not ask this.) If, for example, you're worried about a big financial decision your parent is facing or the ability to drive, try asking the doctor to specifically weigh in on that AND to explain how they came to their conclusion.

- **Keep asking *why*.** Use this key word to react to a diagnosis, prescription, or other recommendation. It's not enough to be told something; you need to understand the thinking behind it and the expected result.

- **Ask the doctor to be more specific about what he or she thinks you should now do** about the concern you've brought up. If they seem reluctant to weigh in specifically on capacity or on a diagnosis, try asking them to be specific about what you and your family should or can do for the time being. If you've brought up that your older father's gotten lost while driving and had a few fender benders but the doctor doesn't seem to think it's time to insist he stop driving, you could ask, "So what do you think we should specifically do to keep him safe while driving? Since he's gotten lost a few times, I'm concerned it might happen again, and I'd like to know what you think we should do to prevent it or what to do if it happens again." You can also ask the doctor to clarify at what point they think something else should be done. For example, "I just want to understand at what point would you say he should stop driving?"

- **Ask about a recommended follow-up.** You shouldn't have to walk out empty-handed with a verdict of "Everything's fine" or "There's nothing else to do." Thank the doctor for the consult but be sure to ask for clarification on next steps: what is the plan for following up and checking on things again?

Even if the doctor just says, "Well, let's see how things go and let me know if anything changes," ask if they think it's a good idea to reevaluate in three to six months (if you think you can live with the status quo until then). They're apt to agree and this might be a way to get your parent to agree to return. In the meantime, carefully document the changes you see. This option only works well if you're just beginning to see changes and think that your parent's current situation is workable for the near future. Obviously, if things decline quickly, you should let the doctor know.

- **Ask about a referral to neurology.** Honestly, we don't love this approach, as experts consistently agree that the recommended steps for an initial cognitive evaluation can and should be doable by primary care providers. That said, many PCPs simply don't feel they have the time or expertise to evaluate cognitive impairment and much prefer to pass this on to a specialist. Instead of trying to persuade a resistant PCP to do all the necessary steps, you might instead just see if they're willing to refer your parent.

- **Seek a second opinion.** It can be tricky to get your parent to consent to another visit if the first doctor found no impairment (especially if it's a longtime doctor). You can try some of the ideas in the section above. Or wait until there's another plausible reason for a checkup (a fall that warrants checking out, an annual flu shot) and try again but with a different doctor. (You could use a fiblet that the regular doctor doesn't have any availability, hence the different doctor.) Meanwhile, document any changes you're seeing and communicate this to the new doctor before the appointment. Be sure you've prepared enough for the appointment by bringing documentation, visit summaries or other records, and medications.

- **Consider going for a more in-depth cognitive assessment at a memory-care clinic.** These practices have specialists (neurologists, psychiatrists, psychologists) and resources to do a more detailed level of evaluation. Ask the doctor you're seeing for a referral.

If the Doctor Alludes to a Dementia Diagnosis But Is Otherwise Unhelpful

This issue is less about an obstacle to getting a diagnosis and more about obstacles to getting a *correctly done* diagnosis and to *getting related help* after a diagnosis. Although it's most common for memory and function to be waved off by busy providers as "just getting old," sometimes they'll go ahead and say that it's probable dementia but that "nothing can be done about it." In either case, you're left still feeling stumped about how to proceed.

Often, these doctors are right when they quickly conclude that the patient has dementia. The condition becomes common as people age so if a family complains of memory problems and paranoia in an 89-year-old, chances are quite high that the older person has dementia.

But there are two big problems with this: First, it's sometimes *not* dementia. It might be a slowly resolving delirium along with a brain-clouding medication. Or depression. Or an infection.

And second, even if it is dementia, it's inaccurate to say that nothing can be done. You want to make sure your parent then gets medical care that fits with the dementia diagnosis and, just as important, you want help address your parent's care needs.

If you're left unsatisfied by a cursory exam or conclusion, what can you do?

Try This:

- **Ask the provider to verify that all other causes and contributors to cognitive impairment you've heard about have been checked for.** Again, if they didn't seem to check all the items that are part of a cognitive evaluation, bring in your worksheet and ask for their help in addressing the items. Remember to be as diplomatic as possible.

- **Ask the provider what impact, if any, a dementia finding has on the rest of the patient's care.** If they have other chronic conditions, will anything be managed differently? Could medications or other aspects of treatment be simplified, given that remembering is getting challenging? Are there other particular issues you should look out for? For example, geriatric experts recommend simplifying insulin regimens for people with dementia who have insulin-requiring diabetes.

- **Realize it's often not particularly helpful to insist providers attempt to diagnose which specific type of dementia it is.** What's more important: Does this seem to be permanent? Should your family expect it to slowly get worse? Have we checked for common medical conditions that make memory and thinking worse? How can we better manage [insert challenging symptom or behavior]? Chasing down the specific type of dementia tends to not be useful because, especially once people are over age 85, most dementia is mixed. Whatever their origins, progressive dementias will continue to progress in ways that similarly require increased family involvement and adapting care to whatever challenging symptoms or behaviors a particular person is experiencing. Also, waiting to get a specific diagnosis often causes delay in getting the education and supportive services that families really need.

- **Look elsewhere for practical help or guidance for dementia caregiving.** This point has to do with reframing your expectations from the doctor. Busy and cure-focused, most doctors have little to offer patients and their families about Alzheimer's and other forms of dementia. This might seem surprising, given that dementia is a fairly common condition. But most health providers are woefully ill-prepared to advise older adults and families on key things to know, like how to meet current care needs, how to manage difficult behaviors, and how to plan for dementia progressing. Unless your parent happens to be getting care from a geriatric clinic or center specializing in dementia, you'll need to look elsewhere for the advice and support you'll need, such as a local Alzheimer's Association chapter. Dr. K's Helping Older Parents courses and online programs are other options. (See RESOURCES.)

- **Consider a second opinion.** It's worth mentioning that this is an option whenever you're left unsatisfied by a medical encounter. It's possible the doctor is not a good fit for you. Be aware, however, that it's fairly rare for the problem to not be dementia at all. The doctor is likely right. Think about whether your dissatisfaction really stems from feeling that you've been left without clarity about what to do next. In that case, your best bet may be to start looking outside the usual medical system for information and support.

If the Doctor Won't Tell You Anything

In some cases, a parent who seems to be having cognitive problems has had an evaluation but won't, or can't, share the results with you. A similar conundrum: You aren't sure what's been done, if anything. Your parent isn't forthcoming. And the doctor won't fill you in either. You're left with little clarity about what's already been done and where things stand. Then what?

Try This:

- **Try to politely remind the provider that HIPAA rules mean it may be possible to share this information with you.** Providers, lacking familiarity with HIPAA nuances, sometimes mistakenly claim that it's impossible for them to talk to family without their patient's express and written consent. But HIPAA's rules and requirements are often misunderstood.

  In fact, HIPAA rules give health providers a lot of leeway in talking to family members.

Providers are *required* to disclose to the patient or their proxy information that's requested. (This is known as "Right of Access.") Other things they are *permitted* to disclose.

Specifically, they're permitted to disclose certain information without obtaining the patient's written or verbal permission—if, using their clinical judgment when a patient lacks capacity to give consent, the clinician decides the disclosure is in the patient's best interests. Naturally, to protect themselves, they should document why they think the patient lacks capacity and why a disclosure is in the patient's interest. They can't just tell you anything but they can decide on a "need to know" basis what's relevant and necessary. An example that illustrates this: The doctor can send all of a patient's medical records to the hospital if her patient is hospitalized; hospital staff would be able to discuss the relevant parts of those records with family members if the person is incapacitated but they wouldn't let you rifle through the person's entire health history.

By the way, written consent, or authorization for the provider to talk to someone other than the patient—known as a waiver—isn't something required under HIPAA regulations. Many offices or providers have this requirement to protect themselves, but it's not a HIPAA requirement.

- **If you or someone else has a durable power of attorney for healthcare for your parent, let the doctor know this.** The person with that authority should be able to obtain the answers you're looking for.

- **Ask whether the provider would be willing to report self-neglect (or other issues) to Adult Protective Services.** In most states, health providers are mandated reporters of elder abuse and self-neglect does count as something that should be reported. If doctors are mandated reporters in your state, consider politely reminding them of this.

- **If neither you nor an ally has durable power of attorney for**

health care:

Bring a copy of the HIPAA rules from the US Department of Health and Human Services website that show a health care provider may disclose protected information to family if the provider determines that the person is incapacitated and it's in his or her best interest that the person involved knows about the patient's care. Many providers are not familiar with HIPAA rules that protect them. (For more about HIPAA, see RESOURCES.)

Or try a different provider. If you're really stuck trying to work with one doctor but are convinced that your parent is acting against their best interests, you may have better luck with someone else who takes a more educated eye to HIPAA rules.

If you are truly stuck, unfortunately you'll have to consider pursuing legal help and potentially guardianship. Alternatively, some families choose to wait until there is a serious health emergency or mental decline that is quite advanced.

If There's Family Disagreement

Family discord about how to proceed typically falls into two main categories:

1. **The roadblock is your parent's partner or spouse,** who may be in denial about cognitive changes taking place and minimize or brush off any concerns you raise. Sometimes one spouse covers up for the other, either intentionally or inadvertently, making it hard to gauge the depth of the problem. Spouses also, of course, "circle the wagons" to protect each other from another generation's perceived interference.

   It's especially challenging, and not uncommon, for a partner to also have cognitive deficits, acknowledged or unacknowledged.

   Whether for these or other reasons, some spouses block any

interference they perceive from adult children, stepchildren, or grandchildren. Complicating matters, the spouse typically is the person with powers of attorney.

2. **The roadblock is a sibling.** Variations here are as plentiful as family arrangements: One sibling may see a problem brewing but another doesn't want to "upset the apple cart" by doing anything about it or is in denial that any problem exists at all. An adult child who lives closer to an older parent often has a harder time seeing cognitive changes than one who sees the parent less often (in which case changes are more apparent). Or vice versa: the nearby child feels a greater sense of urgency than one who drops in less often, when impaired parents often rise to the occasion or the degree of trouble is otherwise masked.

   Step-siblings or half-siblings can add another complicated layer. And don't underestimate the disruptive role that birth order, family history, or other family dynamics can play (like the "baby" not being taken seriously, the "favorite" who can do no wrong, the "responsible oldest" who is always deferred to).

   A sibling with power of attorney can also create tensions, although this tends to be more of an issue at later stages of dementia, when that responsibility kicks in.

Whatever the particulars of your situation, disagreement can make decisions harder or seemingly impossible. What helps?

Try This:

- **Start with recognizing that the simple act of talking about a family member's cognition tends to raise tensions.** That's not to say you shouldn't talk! But it's a reminder why these inter-relationship conversations tend to be difficult. Talking about a possible problem generates tension because it brings up the "elephants in the room"—the worries, fears, and other emotions about a situation that otherwise simmer undisturbed.

Remembering this can help you avoid pigeon-holing relatives as "difficult," "selfish," "unhelpful," and so on. Chances are, they're actually afraid of the fear, anxiety, or change that talking forces to the forefront.

- **Double down on good communication basics.** Step back. Ask open-ended questions rather than just stating what you think should be done: "I'm noticing a lot more forgetfulness in Mom, what do you think about it?" "What worries you most about Dad not being able to drive anymore?" "Do you wonder what will happen when this house gets to be too much?"

Encourage other family to express their own fears and concerns. Remember that each party has a unique and separate relationship to a parent. You're not all the same. Even if you don't agree with or act on everything said, simply listening moves you closer to collaboration.

- **As you listen, try to figure out how they see the situation and what their fears and desires are.** By doing so, you can frame your suggestions in ways that make it easier for them to accept your ideas. Do they feel threatened by a possible loss of control? "What would you like to see happen? I'd like to help make things easier for you." Are they afraid of a living situation changing? "I know you love this house; have you thought about...?" Are they acting out of habit, like old sibling rivalry that just hates the idea of you being "right" (and making them feel "wrong")? "I know we have a lot of old differences but let's agree to put Mom first for now."

- **Be transparent and keep key players in the loop.** Often, resistance or disagreement stems simply from not having all the facts or feeling left out. Find what works best for your family: Group meetings, calls, or text chats? A standing weekly 1:1? Keep written records of doctor appointments, expenditures, research, and anything else you do to help your parent. This is not only a source of knowledge for everyone involved but can protect you against later attacks.

- **Separate the biggies from the small stuff.** Families aren't likely to agree on everything. You might have to let small matters go so you can focus on the big things.

- **Seek advice from neutral outsiders.** Sometimes you can break an impasse by getting input on your situation from an online care group, friends, a clergyperson, or a family elder. Your own family member may be more receptive to an idea coming from a third party. (Note: this can also backfire if your family member is sensitive to "airing dirty laundry" by taking your situation outside the immediate family circle so consider who you're dealing with.)

- **Have a professional facilitate a few family conversations.** Certain professionals, such as some geriatric care managers and professional elder mediators, are skilled at mediating conversations between people in close relationships, especially concerning aging and eldercare. On one level, their value can be simple acknowledgement that, "Yes, this is an issue that needs addressing." That's useful when you're dealing with denial. And on another level, they're extremely knowledgeable about local resources and how to create an action plan. When things are really fractious, a third-party expert can be a real icebreaker.

TIP: Ideally, if you, another family member, and your parent live in different cities, find a care manager or mediator in your parent's community to start.

If You Lack the Legal Tools to Help

As we explained in Chapter 4, you'll have more options available to help your parent if you or someone in your family has been designed durable power of attorney for both healthcare and general affairs. (Remember, they're two different documents.)

If your parents are trustees of their own living trust, this usually names a successor trustee and explains under what circumstances the trustees should be considered incapacitated so that successor trustees can act.

If your parents haven't completed power of attorney documents, we explain your options in Chapter 4, in this section: If your parent hasn't named you (or anyone else) in a power of attorney document.

Basically, you'll want to consider whether you or someone in the family might be able to persuade them to complete a POA. Otherwise, you'll just have to work with the other tools we've described in this book, such as communication, attempting gentle persuasion, coordinating with your parent's health professionals when possible, leveraging other influencers in your parent's life, and tapping into whatever local resources are available to assist families and older adults.

We've described many local resources in this book but in general, the places we recommend you start looking are:

- Your local Area Agency on Aging

- Family Caregiver Alliance Navigator

- Local nonprofits that help older adults in your parent's area

If Your Parent Doesn't Want *Any* Help

What if your parent completely pushes back on any involvement or assistance of any kind from you? Then what?

Everything is harder in this situation. Not that your parent will necessarily see it this way. Reasons for refusal are plentiful. To name a few: Pride and dignity, a fierce sense of "not your business," stoicism about managing alone and wanting to maintain control, the power of habit, fears they don't want to share with children, relational concerns (lack of trust, a fractious history, wariness about your motives), or a lack of insight about the probable need for help due to cognitive problems, depression, or another ailment.

If this comes up for you, we recommend focusing on three considerations:

1. **Whether the difficulties you're observing are significant enough to qualify as "self-neglect."**

2. **Whether anyone else is being put at risk, for example by dangerous driving or an impaired spousal caregiver.**

3. **Whether the capacity issues are bad enough to consider "desperate measures" such as looking into guardianship.**

If the answers to these three questions are "No" or "Probably not," you'll need to focus your efforts on trying to build up a positive connection with your parent, giving persuasion another try in the future, and otherwise standing by until things get worse. The following suggestions cover some of this.

If, on the other hand, you think your answers to the questions above are "Yes" or "Maybe," you'll also want to give hard consideration to the final two points listed below.

Try This:

- **Realize that it's "the norm" for older adults to live in risky suboptimal circumstances for months to years.** It's not ideal and we wish things were different. *You* will wish things were different! But in our vast experience, this uncomfortable state is true. The main reasons: 1) There's a gray area for both capacity and self-neglect (remember, these things are not always clear-cut), and 2) There's a shortage of trained professionals to work with older adults and families, and public programs are underfunded.

  It's theoretically possible to pull together an excellent capable team to help an older person who seems to be at risk; at a minimum you'd want a really good geriatric social worker and a good medical provider trained in geriatrics. And they'd both be able to come to the house, and they'd have the needed communication skills to build trust with your parent and get important things done.

In practice, however? It's extremely hard to find this kind of help, let alone afford it.

The net result is that families are left to rely on the usual "system," which means it's typically very hard to put supports in place for an aging adult at risk until things get pretty bad. In our experience, families who do manage to successfully intervene early, before things get dire, are either lucky (their older parent is more amenable to help than most) or they're able to recruit some excellent professionals to help them (which can be expensive) or they do a lot of hard, persistent work on their own.

More often, while families are in this gray zone, they wind up watching and waiting for the other shoe to drop. It's stressful and can feel unnaturally counter to the strong, well-intentioned drive adult children have to *Do Something*.

- **Consider whether you're attempting to take over issues that are still your parent's responsibility.** It's common for people to want their aging parents to be as safe and healthy as possible. It's also common for older adults to not be doing everything they could to remain safe and well. But here's the thing: Unless your parent is gravely impaired and the job of overseeing their care has been taken over by you, **it's not your job to ensure their safety or well-being.** Your job is to be concerned and to offer whatever help you're able to provide.

  Otherwise, unless you've either been awarded guardianship or have effectively taken over supervising various aspects of their care, you're not responsible. So don't put too much pressure on yourself. And realize that, often, this journey requires accepting that someone we love is making choices we wish they wouldn't make or that the situation is not what we wish it were.

- **Re-evaluate how you're approaching the situation.** Check in with things from your side: Are you practicing good communication skills, including trying to see goals and priorities from your parent's point of view? Are you taking care to validate his or her feelings about the situation? Are you making clear that you're operating from a place of love and concern?

Especially when someone shows cognitive impairment, it becomes even more critical to avoid arguing or "trying to get them to understand." Instead, you want to be even more focused on being a good listener, validating emotions, and projecting cooperation and calm. That's because with cognitive challenges, upsetting feelings can be magnified, causing the stressed person to pull back, dig in, or lash out. If needed, revisit the communication tips in Chapter 2.

- **Consider creative "side door" approaches to how you offer assistance.** Try these tactics in addition to good basic communication. For example, you could propose a change as "temporary:" "What if we tried x for a month or two and see how it goes?" "This company offers a six-week free trial; it doesn't cost anything to cancel so what's to lose?" Maybe you peg a fix like visits from an elder companion or meal delivery "while I'm out of town." Similarly, try offering a service or solution as a gift. If a meal service would be objected to, what about a month of "special Sunday dinner delivery" or a cleaning service pitched as pampering?

- **Consider involving a trained expert to talk to your parent.** Adult children sometimes resist this step because they think that "helping" is something they ought to do themselves. But a good geriatric care manager/aging care specialist, elder law attorney, money manager, or family counselor (especially those who specialize in older populations) is skilled at navigating these conversations. They can help get over impasses when goals are clashing (for instance, your parent prizes independence; you want them to be safe). These professionals also can help your parent feel heard and "take the heat off" you, moving an adversarial relationship back into more neutral territory, which may make it easier for your parent to be more accepting of your suggestions.

Try pitching it as, "Since we don't agree on this, and I'd like to make sure we're doing what we can to keep you living at home for as long as possible, let's ask this expert for ideas." Many older adults are more open to hearing advice from an expert than their own offspring.

If your parent still refuses, nothing's stopping you from seeking a consultation on your own to get an expert's ideas on what can be tried.

- **Think hard to get some clarity (for your own sake as much as your parent's) about what's driving your desire to push for help**. Is it your fear of a possible disaster? Your deep desire to "do the right thing" in "taking care of" your parent? Your irritation over unsafe or unwise ways your parent manages their life?

Think hard about what kind of help your parent actually NEEDS (in contrast to what you WANT to provide). Ultimately, even someone with dementia has preferences and those should be honored whenever possible—at least up until the point they're a danger to themselves or others.

TOOL: REVISIT THE ME VS. THEM EXERCISE (IN CHAPTER 4)

- **Realize that you might need to shift from "prevention mode" to "reaction mode."** Obviously, it's better to prevent problems before they happen. But if you're unable to make headway in the ways you'd prefer to avoid future trouble, consider this: You may need to get comfortable with a certain amount of *que sera, sera* in cases where your parent isn't behaving in ways that maybe aren't optimal but also aren't quite dangerous or is making poor choices (or choices you wouldn't make) that may carry some risk but aren't endangering others. In this category:

things like taking medicine haphazardly, not following through on physical rehab, delaying decisions, keeping lots of clutter in the house, refusing to use hearing aids or a walker, even bathing less often than you'd prefer.

In other words, there are less urgent matters and more urgent matters. When resistance itself is becoming a problem, pick your battles.

This is a huge point. We see families beat their heads against the proverbial wall over and over when it's just not the best use of their energy.

Two big categories where you *would* need to be more forceful about a parent refusing help are when they're a threat to themselves or to others (for example, though dangerous driving or forgetfulness that causes them to not safely operate a stove or firearms). Which brings us to these other two measures:

1. **Explore if your parent's difficulties might qualify as self-neglect and consider reporting to Adult Protective Services.** Self-neglect is a term that most states define as some form of inability to adequately provide for one's "self-care," which at a minimum means providing oneself with adequate nourishment, clothing, shelter, and health care. In virtually all states, self-neglect is considered a form of "elder abuse" and is eligible for reporting to Adult Protective Services.

    Just as with capacity, it's fairly common for older adults to fall within a "gray area" when it comes to self-care and whether it's being "neglected" enough to warrant intervention. Especially when it comes to health care, plenty of people don't follow their doctors' recommendations or otherwise fail to get medical care that's often recommended for their situation but usually we don't call Adult Protective Services on them. Still, in most cases, self-neglect involves an older adult having difficulty providing for more than one aspect of their care and well-being.

If you think your parent's difficulties might qualify as self-neglect, then it's more important to attempt to act, even if they're reluctant. A reasonable first step is to contact Adult Protective Services; in most states, they won't reveal your identity to your older parent. It can be a good idea to first see if you can run your parent's situation past a social worker or other professional with expertise on self-neglect to see if they agree that a report to APS is warranted.

Last but not least: In many states, social workers and health providers are "mandated reporters." So if your parent's situation is worrisome but you're reluctant to be the person reporting them, one option is to see if you can get a mandated reporter to do it.

2. **Explore whether your parent's difficulties and capacity issues are bad enough to meet criteria for guardianship in their state**. At this point, we're not suggesting you actually embark on this kind of "desperate measure." But if you're feeling very stuck with a parent who just won't accept help, then it may be a good time to learn more about what IS considered grounds for guardianship in your parent's state.

    This varies from state to state but often requires the person to be demonstrating a substantial inability to manage their finances, housing, or health. The courts will often want to see actual proof that the person has failed in these respects, e.g. actually lost money, really jeopardized their housing, or been hospitalized due to their impaired abilities.

    To learn more about how bad things have to be to qualify for guardianship, the best information will come from a knowledgeable elder law attorney. But you can often get your research started less expensively by talking to social workers and geriatric care managers; just be sure to confirm they have experience with guardianship cases involving older adults in your parent's jurisdiction.

In the meantime: Keep taking notes on what you see your parent struggling with. This will come in handy if ever your family does end up considering guardianship.

What This Looks Like:
The Smiths and The Johnsons

Example 1: The Smiths

Zeke, the son, felt frustrated after accompanying his father to his doctor's appointment. The doctor didn't seem to check his cognition, either at this meeting or in the past. Given the family's concerns about Albert's capacity to continue driving and managing his finances, among other things, and the fact that he had a springing POA, Zeke really needed the doctor to weigh in.

He decided to try again. First, Zeke called the office to double-check whether the letter he'd sent earlier outlining the siblings' concerns about their father's memory and judgment had been received. He discovered something not uncommon: The letter arrived but hadn't been put in his father's file so the doctor never saw it. Zeke asked for it to be shown to him as well as to talk to the doctor by phone. In the call, he explained the specific issues the family had been seeing and said they were worried about Albert's capacity to safely drive and manage finances.

"I'm not asking you to reveal anything right now or explain what you think is going on," he stressed. "I'm just asking how you might be able to help us with these issues." This kind of specific ask is often effective; indeed, Albert's doctor said he'd call Albert back in on the pretext of getting some overlooked lab work done, along with a blood pressure recheck. During the exam, he'll do a quick cognitive check, telling Albert that it's something he's now doing with all his older patients.

This happened quickly. The doctor determined that Albert is showing signs of cognitive impairment, though seems unaware of this, and said he'd reassess him in three months. Although he wasn't ready to confirm incapacity for finances, he agreed that driving could be problematic. He advised Albert to hold off on driving "for now," saying that he thought that vision and a few other medical issues needed to be checked. In a private aside to Zeke, the doctor also offered to file a report with the DMV.

Before Albert could even make a fuss over this, he had another accident. Fortunately, he wasn't hurt badly but his car needed major repairs. The siblings agreed to fudge the truth and tell him it wasn't salvageable. Zeke came to stay with his dad for a few weeks to handle the transportation needed for food and doctor visits. The doctor told Albert he needs to stop driving and Albert didn't protest. It's become clear, though, that Albert can't keep living alone—which Albert vigorously resists.

Meanwhile, Zeke's sister was able to hire a geriatric care manager. They explained to Albert that she's the friend of a friend who lives in his same town, and it would make them feel better just to know he had someone younger he could call for any help needed. He agreed to meet with her. The GCM broke the tension with several suggestions:

- She empathized with Albert over his driving troubles. She said things like, "Oh, I broke my ankle once and couldn't drive; it's so maddening to have to figure out how to get around, isn't it? Let's think about how you can get around." By showing the siblings how to join in his frustration, she was able to turn a situation where Albert felt demeaned and the kids were digging in their heels to keep him safe into one of collaboration. Instead of making it sound like his independence was being taken away, she sounded like she was helping him solve a problem without making him feel bad about himself.

- That paved the way for her to introduce ideas "just for now" that could be longer-term solutions, to which Albert was now more receptive. He agreed to her arranging a car service that could take him to the diner or the store. She also suggested that he might want to think about hiring "an assistant" who could shop and cook for him, to make it more convenient to get the good meals he enjoyed. He agreed. The person hired, who came in three mornings a week, was actually a caregiver who would also keep an eye on how Albert was doing generally.

- By introducing this relationship, the geriatric care manager set the stage for there to be an "outsider" Albert trusted who could deliver more help as needed.

Example 2: The Johnsons

Sue Johnson is eager to get her mother, Maria, to a medical consult but Maria has refused to go. Sue is pretty sure that her mother has probable dementia, although she's also read that depression can cause memory problems. Sue's sense is that her mother knows something's wrong but is afraid to find out. Sue thinks the cognitive changes are also preventing her mom from thinking clearly.

Because of all this, Sue feels justified in trying a little deception to get her mother the checkup she needs. Sue contacts her own doctor and explains the situation, including that Maria is terrified of having dementia because of her best friend's experience and avoids most medical care generally.

They agree that Sue will bring Maria in for a flu shot, during which the doctor will also try to do some cognitive evaluation, including a check for clinical depression. To get her mom to agree to even this much, Sue uses another pretext, that her child's doctor is recommending grandparents get flu shots to be around their grandchildren this year. She knows Maria will do anything for her grandson.

This plan works. Not only that but Maria likes the doctor. So Maria takes it well when the new doctor expresses affectionate surprise that

Maria hasn't had any other regular care in years. Saying that he knows Maria lost her husband, which must take a toll on how she feels, he suggests that it's smart to get in her best condition in order to be there for her grandson. Seeing Maria hesitate, Sue chimes in that "with all the insurance and paperwork that Dad used to take care of but doesn't now," a physical will probably be needed soon anyway.

Maria relents. Once she establishes a relationship with Sue's doctor, several successive visits confirm that she's in generally good physical health, except for a thyroid condition and some arthritis, but that there are cognitive concerns. The doctor also thinks Maria does have some mild symptoms of depressed mood and endorses the idea of a grief support group, which Maria likes, also recommends more time with family, which she clearly seems to enjoy, and regular physical activity. As far as the changes in her memory and thinking skills, the doctor assures Maria that there's no need to worry that everything will change overnight; she's still the same patient who walked in the door.

Because Sue got her mother to name her in powers of attorney documents, she's able to have conversations with the doctor about Maria's cognitive status. Sue feels relieved to have confirmation of what's going on—though she's worried about what's ahead.

PART FOUR: TAKING THE LONG VIEW

**BRACE FOR A MARATHON OF UPS AND DOWNS AS YOU CON-
TINUE YOUR EFFORTS TO HELP (ALMOST ALWAYS LASTING
LONGER THAN YOU EXPECT)**

We've provided the basic formula for intervening in your aging parent's life when you start seeing signs that they may need help. You can apply, and reapply, these ideas as long as they're needed.

Consider yourself forewarned: they may be needed for quite a while.

Situations with older adults who need help are rarely one-fix-and-done, much as we'd like it to be that way. You may think you've hit on a solution, only to have it never get off the ground because of resistance, a worsening condition, or some other factor you can't control. Or you set something up and it falls apart. Things may proceed in a semi-stable way for some months or years, only to collapse in the face of some kind of new crisis. Stuff happens.

Frankly, it can wear you down.

Plus, as time goes on, your parents are almost certainly going to decline and eventually need more help.

This section is intended to address the long view.

In Chapter 7, we address the logistics of figuring out what you can do when progress seems stalled (or moving backward). How will you know if it's time to change course? What's a practical way to manage over the long haul?

In Chapter 8, we'll cover an all-too-often overlooked dimension of all this: setting yourself up for what is likely to be a journey of at least a few years, helping your parent navigate age-related declines.

Please don't skip this info. This journey inevitably brings ongoing stress and uncertainty but it IS possible to make it more manageable so you can sustain a journey of years with less risk of burnout. Without paying some attention to your own care and approach to all this, you risk a lot of unnecessary frustration or even health problems and repercussions to your work, relationships, and other responsibilities. We promise we won't just tell you to "make time for bubble baths and lots of sleep!" (which, admittedly, is the usual impractical self-care advice often doled out to those providing care).

Together, these chapters are meant to sustain you through the long stretch of the journey of helping an older parent—and its toll on your time and patience.

Chapter 7:
Try This When You Feel Really Stuck

If at first you don't succeed…you experiment and try again. In fact, "try and try again" may well be the motto of helping an older parent. As we've suggested repeatedly in the previous chapters, it's a journey requiring a lot of perseverance. Fine-tuning your attempts is to be expected because it's hard to hit the mark perfectly the first time you try something. We call this repeated iteration "giving things a good try."

But sometimes even a really good try goes nowhere. Despite your best efforts (good communication, thorough research, creative thinking, reflecting, attempting new approaches to obstacles), you may still not feel like you're making progress. Things are at real impasse.

That can be really wearing.

It's seldom your fault, especially if you've put the time, thought, and energy into going through the steps we've mapped out. Experts in aging agree that as a society, we don't have enough trained professionals and available programs to support older adults in later life—and to help older adults and their families navigate challenges when abilities start to slip. Plus, your specific situation could be complicated by any number of things—an intensely private or obstinate parent, limited resources where they live, an elusive diagnosis, a lack of family unity, insufficient paperwork, and so on.

When you reach such a crossroads, you have a few options.

This stage is different from continuing to experiment with alternatives (making slight changes, like trying a different home care agency, using a new persuasive approach, or giving your parent a little space before revisiting a topic). It usually involves a bigger shift in strategy—and a shift in your thinking.

Here are some ways forward from "stuck:"

Reassess What's Happened So Far

Just as reviewing what's not working is a key part of iterating your attempts to help an older parent, it's equally important to take stock when you feel you're still not getting anywhere after multiple efforts.

Your goal now: To step back a bit and review the bigger picture of what you've been hoping to address and whether it's a good idea to keep working on it. That can help you decide whether, and how, to pivot.

Start here:

- **Review your communication with your parent.** Did he or she not respond to any of the communication tips in Chapters 2 and 4? Do you have any insight into why? (Maybe your parent lacks the capacity to be rational, for example. Maybe your history makes it hard for you to find the patience required.)

- **Review the intervention you came up with:** Was it grounded in the ideal next steps described in Chapter 3? Have you done enough research about your options to feel confident that they're plausible for your parent's situation (whether you had any success with them or not)?

- **Use the Me vs. Them tool** (at the end of Chapter 4) to get some insight into any differences between you and your parent that might help shed light on why things aren't working.

- **Review the steps you've chosen to act on and the experimenting you've done to make them happen** (Chapter 5). Remember, after you go through the A-B-C-D-E formula of deciding how to intervene, it's inevitable to have to do so a few times. Consider whether you've tried the tips for common obstacles found in Chapter 6. If none of these things seems to be helping, what do you think are the stumbling blocks?

The purpose of stepping back and going through this thought process is to understand how you got to this point of frustration and to make sure you haven't overlooked something.

Also: It can be reassuring to remind yourself that you've done everything within your control that you can reasonably do. That still won't solve the problem but it puts you in a healthier frame of mind for what might come next.

Consider a Different Strategy or Issue to Address

Another option when you're stuck is to set aside what you've been trying to do and switch your focus to another direction. Is there a different way you can help your parent?

This isn't experimenting with alternatives—coming at the same problem in a new way. If you've been following our approach, you've been there and done that already. This is trying to do something else altogether. Chances are that there are a number of issues your parent needs help with, large and small. Tackling one of these, for now, can satisfy your sense of progress. In a very practical way, you're still helping your parent achieve a better quality of life, more safety, better health or function, even if it's not the issue you see as a top priority.

Go back to the brainstorming exercise you did in Chapter 5 (the "B" in the A-B-C-D-E formula). You probably came up with a list of things to be done. Pick another one and try that. Set aside, for now, the issue you're getting nowhere with.

Consider "Watchful Waiting"

Sometimes you reach a point where the best thing to do is not to intervene in a different or new way but to actually stop intervening. Hit pause.

We call this "watchful waiting." Its origins in medicine mean to let some time pass before a treatment or other intervention. During that time, we monitor the situation to see what happens (new symptoms, improvement, or decline) while avoiding possible negative effects of stepping in.

In helping an aging parent, you may reach a point where there's nothing else you can do but watch and wait. It can feel like "waiting for the other shoe to drop." But it's not the same as doing nothing.

It's a carefully considered decision made after deliberately assessing the situation and having tried various options without making headway.

You might choose this course of action if:

- Your suggestions have been repeatedly ignored.

- All help has been actively rebuffed or refused.

- Your parent's mental or physical state is declining but they retain capacity and enough function to manage okay.

- You've realized you're worried about a future possible event (a fall, an accident) rather than an actual crisis now.

- The risks of intervening (an unhappy parent, a fractured relationship) outweigh the benefits (what you see as safety but your parent sees as interference).

- No one in the family can agree what to do and there's no urgent problem.

- A medical evaluation for dementia was inconclusive and your parent seems to have capacity to call the shots.

Remember, though, your ultimate role isn't to fix everything or to "get them to do" anything. (Even if that's your natural mode.) It's to honor your parent's preferences and respect and support their autonomy as best as circumstances allow. The essence of helping an older parent is that you're traveling the journey through this phase of life with them, not efficiently rushing to any particular destination. (And especially not rushing them to the destination that YOU think is right for them.)

HOW TO FEEL BETTER ABOUT WATCHFUL WAITING:

Even so, this strategy can create intense discomfort in an adult child. You might think, "I'm being neglectful!" That's a perfectly natural response. But if you've taken all the earlier steps, it's more of an emotional response than a logical one. It's risky, but sometimes necessary, to make a choice you know will leave you feeling guilty, unsupportive, or inadequate (however unfounded those feelings are).

Know that you'll probably need to keep working on acknowledging these feelings and reprogramming them.

How?

- Recognize that "doing nothing" as a strategy at this point is different from having never noticed your parent needed help and having never done anything to try to address that need. You've been doing plenty for a while now.

- Recognize that the "doing nothing" is in large part in service to respecting your parent's wishes and dignity.

- Realize, too, that you're not really doing absolutely nothing even now. You're standing by (the "watchful" part of "watchful waiting").

- Meanwhile, you can still play an active role, if you want, in many ways:

  - You can focus on building your connection with your parent. It's time you may be grateful for later and can build goodwill that may make decision-making easier in the event of a crisis.

- You can spend pleasurable time together (if doing so doesn't drive either of you crazy), which can improve quality of life all around.

- You can set up whatever assists or small fixes will be accepted.

- You can keep checking in with how things are going and how your parent is feeling about it.

- You can check in with other family members for their perspectives and ideas.

- You can continue to research "what if" options.

- You can take care of yourself so you're better able to stay mentally and physically healthy when or if things should worsen.

Some of you may be concerned that watchful waiting leaves you liable to neglect. Unless you're already your parent's legal guardian or conservator, or have a fiduciary role, this is very unlikely. You may want to look up your state's statutes concerning elder abuse and neglect. But for most of the situations we're describing, most people shouldn't worry about a legal dimension to stepping back to a more hands-off approach.

While this approach may be uncomfortable for you, it can buy time and peace. We hope it also brings you a certain amount of reassurance. It's a reminder that you've been trying and you're doing your best. When and if a crisis does occur, you can react to that changed set of circumstances.

Consider "Desperate Measures"

Sometimes what's in order is a difficult action that you'd prefer not to take. Or as the saying goes, "Desperate times call for desperate measures."

This is usually a last-resort approach, typically if your parent lacks capacity and is no longer willing or able to act in their own best interest AND if they are actually experiencing significant life consequences due to their incapacity. If you feel your parent is endangering himself (or endangering others), if an emergency happens and you don't know what else to do, or if you've exhausted other efforts, you may need to consider desperate measures.

Some examples:

- Reporting a dangerous driver to the DMV or disabling their vehicle.

- Reporting your parent's situation to Adult Protective Services if you suspect elder abuse and/or self-neglect.

- Using deception to move a parent without capacity to a safer living situation.

- Petitioning for guardianship (Chapter 4).

- Bringing legal action against your parent or another party (like a family member or aide you feel is acting inappropriately or is financially exploiting your parent).

- Calling 911 if you feel your parent is in imminent danger (losing control, behaving erratically, endangering themselves or others).

As you can see, this strategy falls along a spectrum. That's because we're all different. For some people, hiding the car keys might feel drastic, while for others, a last resort is more along the lines of taking legal action. What the situations tend to have in common is that the action would make the parent—and often other family members—really up-set. And that, of course, makes this choice all the more fraught.

Before you take what you consider to be a last-approach step, it's smart to talk to others who are familiar with the action. Ask other caregivers if they have done such a thing. Seek the advice of a geriatric care manager or other relevant professional. You want to find out the potential pitfalls, best ways to go about it, and other helpful advice.

What This Looks Like:
The Smiths and The Johnsons

Example 1: The Smiths

Albert recovered from his latest car wreck (luckily the car was more damaged than he was). He settled back into his old routines, with some new changes suggested by the geriatric care manager his children had hired. The "assistant" does his shopping and cooks meals several days a week for him. He seems to enjoy having the company, and she has also begun driving him to his barbershop.

But he often forgets why he no longer can drive (doctor's orders) and becomes angry. He also keeps offering to write the aide big checks for no reason. He has also asked her to buy a car for him to replace the one that was wrecked. His son, Zeke, has begun visiting more often and sees that there are more unpaid bills; he worries about late fees and missed payments. Albert steadfastly refuses any more help.

Zeke gets back in touch with Albert's primary care doctor to report the latest. As promised, the doctor has been seeing Albert more of-ten to monitor his cognition. He has concluded that Albert does have dementia. He explains this to his patient and reminds him of his pre-scription to give up driving, although none of this seems to register with Albert. The doctor provides the letter Zeke needs to activate his springing powers of attorney. Now, at least, he can take steps to further monitor his father's use of funds and pay his bills—although he can't prevent him entirely from spending large sums. (A power of attorney for finances allows you to do certain things, but it doesn't stop the other person from doing things.) Indeed, he tried hiding the checkbook from Albert, but Albert just ordered a replacement.

Meanwhile, Zeke asks the geriatric care manager whether they should consider guardianship in order to bring about the changes their father needs. She explains that in their state, it can be difficult and expensive to take this step, and given their situation, Albert is liable to feel demeaned and angry by this step. Instead, she recommends a more discreet approach to protect Albert's finances from himself, which is talking to the bank manager directly. He brings his power of attorney for finances, which is now activated, and additional documentation (a letter) from the doctor explaining what's going on. It turns out that longtime employees at the bank who know Albert have noticed his memory loss and other changes. The bank sets up a new account in Albert's name (but managed by Zeke) that keeps a maximum of $500 in it at all times; Zeke gives Albert a checkbook for this account. Albert's other assets are kept in his preexisting account, which Zeke continues to monitor and manage, acting as Albert's attorney.

Meanwhile, Zeke also makes an appointment with an elder law attorney to get her take on guardianship. She agrees with the geriatric care manager that the bar is very high to prove this and that other financial measures, such as managing his accounts for him, may be effective enough. The attorney advises that Albert's main asset, his house, is protected under a trust, which Zeke is now able to arrange on Albert's behalf.

Zeke and his siblings feel proud they've been able to keep Albert in his own home with a sense of independence and dignity. All this effort has not been easy, however. In fact, it feels like they're propping up a house of cards—one fall or other mishap away from the current arrangements falling apart. Albert has steadfastly refused to move in with one of his children and for various reasons this doesn't seem to be a workable solution for the future. But what about assisted living? Because Zeke has access now to his father's paperwork, he thinks he can make the numbers work. The siblings go back to the process in Chapter 5 and map out how they might do this, researching places, consulting with the geriatric care manager, and brainstorming how they could get Albert to agree to moving if and when it's needed.

Example 2: The Johnsons

Maria's diagnosis of probable dementia has made Sue feel slightly better—at least she knows what she's dealing with—but Maria feels worse. She's scared. She shuts down a little bit and insists she doesn't want help or "pity."

Sue does as much as she can: Automating payments for her mom, regularly reducing clutter, signing her up for Meals on Wheels, and enlisting an old friend to take her to the senior center for a crafting afternoon she enjoys. She also sets up a weekly date for Maria and her son. She tries to make sure she's taking her new medications.

It's all exhausting, though. Sue has her own home and family to look after. She finds that she worries constantly about whether Maria is turning off the stove, leaving shoes where she'll trip, or remembering to eat. She wishes she'd get out more. She'd like Maria to move in with her but her mom is adamant. No. Anytime Sue tries to bring it up, Maria starts to yell at her.

With hard reflection, Sue decides that Maria is taking a lot of comfort from being in her own home around familiar things. She's willing to have Sue's family help her and seems grateful for their assistance. Her world is small but manageable. Although bad things might happen, Sue knows that things aren't too bad yet. Over the past few months, her mom has actually seemed happier, perhaps because she's now spending time with her grandson and other people more regularly. Sue feels like she's not doing "enough" and knows she'll feel terrible if her mom falls or, as her mother's friend May once did, wanders away from home. At the same time, she knows (and her husband keeps reminding her) that she has thoughtfully considered all the options for her mother and has done so much already. She's not doing "nothing" about her mom's safety issues; she's doing "watchful waiting" and is starting to work on a plan for how they could move Maria if/when things get worse. She can't control everything. She's being the good daughter she wants to be.

Chapter 8: Equip Yourself for the Longer Journey of Helping Your Aging Parent

Most of what people go through to help an aging parent aren't over-and-done sprints—they're marathons. Across the many variables in family situations, we see one theme pretty consistently: stress, fatigue, and worry along the way.

It's almost inevitable: The very definition of aging is a process of change. Growing older involves increasing frailty and new challenges. You all have to roll with the punches. The nature and pace of these changes is unpredictable, though, no matter how much planning you do.

There are ways to lessen the stress if you can be a little proactive (which, admittedly, isn't a mode that comes naturally to most of us), and if you can think about how to pace yourself, so that you can accompany your parent on this journey in the ways that matter the most, for whatever the length of the journey.

As you move forward, a few mindsets become especially useful.

Be Kinder to Yourself

When we're helping another person, it's understandable, even necessary, that they're the focus. The challenge is that helping an older parent often continues for weeks, months, years, or decades. That's a long time—too long—to ignore your own needs, including the other relationships in your life.

It should go without saying that you'll be better equipped to deal in the long run if you find ways to meet your own basic health needs (nutrition, exercise, sleep, checkups) that support you rather than stress you.

Just as important, and often overlooked: give some TLC to your self-image.

When things are stressful or not going smoothly, it's easy to put all the focus on the negative: *I must be doing something wrong. I'm not doing enough. Why can't I get it right?* You may be hearing this kind of criticism from your parent or from other relatives. You might even blame yourself for problems that just happen completely apart from your efforts (because things just happen; that's the nature of the beast): Mom falls. Dad refuses to quit driving and winds up two states away from home. An aide quits. Dementia worsens.

Being more compassionate toward yourself grows only MORE important the longer you're involved in your parent's health and care.

The following tools can help you do this.

TOOL: KINDER SELF-TALK

Language has power. Remind yourself of the following often, even if you have to post notecards on your refrigerator or keep a list in your phone:

I'm doing the best I can.

My best is good enough.

I have needs, too, that deserve to be met.

It's not selfish to put myself first.

My parent isn't the only relationship in my life that merits attention.

I can only do what I can do.

I can research help, propose help, and advocate for my parent to help change the outcome; I can't force my parent or the situation to change.

My parent's well-being, health, and safety aren't measures of my affection or ability.

Sometimes just being together with my parent is more important than doing things for him or her.

TOOL: FLIP TO THE POSITIVE

An unfortunate side effect of stress is that we revert to negative ways of framing our thoughts. And then our minds start to believe that story rather than a different reality.

Consciously try to flip what you think and say to a positive. In every case, it's possible:

Instead of: "I messed up."

Say: "That didn't work; I'll try something else."

Instead of: "I don't have time to [exercise/make that phone call/see a friend]."

Say: "I have 10 minutes to [get in some exercise/make the call/touch base with my friend]."

Instead of: "I'm really bad at confrontation."

Say: "I'm good at noticing what Dad needs."

OUR FAVORITE SELF-CARE HACKS

More good ways to be kinder to yourself include these:

- **Outsourcing.** Figuring out what tasks or responsibilities you can outsource. Can you pay someone else to handle any of it?

- **Mindfulness/relaxation.** Learning how to practice mindfulness or another relaxation technique. See resources.

- **Sleep.** If you're having trouble with it, address it to stem future physical or mental health problems and to extend your patience with your parent. The solution might be as simple as a white-noise machine, a weighted blanket, stopping electronics after dinner, or a sleep app.

- **Venting.** Find the outlet that works for you to offload the complex emotions that this work can stir up. Many people we work with have success with journaling, seeing a talk therapist, in-person or online support groups, or spiritual outlets. Notice these are all nonmedical ways to cope with stress (exercise is another great one). Try not to rely on sleep medicines, alcohol, cigarettes, emotional eating, or similar problematic outlets to cope with your aging parent.

- **Intentional time for yourself.** Plan time to restore yourself at regular intervals. Okay, probably it won't be bubble baths every night. Or ever. But really: You can't be there in the ways that are most important for your parent if you let yourself get burnt out. Break time just for you down into specific intervals so you're more likely to follow through: Plan what you'll do daily, weekly, monthly, and annually (or semiannually). Start small if that's all you think you can manage (10 minutes a day to read, a weekly visit with a friend, a monthly haircut) but for each time interval, plan *something*.

Improve Family Dynamics

Another thing that helps in the long haul but often isn't paid attention to is the broader family, not just your parent in need:

- Your other parent(s)

- Your siblings

- Your partner

- Other relatives

- Other relationships in your life

They can seem like another source of stress. Or they can be a resource for you. Whenever there's a crisis, you can count on family tensions to flare up. The more you work on collaboration and communication in an ongoing way, the more relationship capital you have to rely on when emergencies happen.

Try to prioritize:

- **Ongoing transparency.** A lot of family rancor can be avoided by lifting the cloak of mystery about finances, medical updates, legal documents, and other key information. If you think a fellow family member would want to know a piece of info, they probably would. They'll be less inclined to hold things against you or take action against you if they've been made to feel part of the process all along. You hate to think the worst of family members but financial matters in particular can wrench people apart. Better to be proactive.

- **Frequent communication.** Even when everything feels calm and stable, it's useful to continue to update all the key stakeholders in your family. Whether you use emails, a group chat, calls, or in-person catch-ups, it's helpful to continue to solicit their views on how things are going and suggestions for how to improve things.

- **Respecting others' relationships.** It bears repeating that every family member, from a spouse to a child to another relative, has a unique connection to your parent that you can't begin to fully understand. Even if you wind up doing the lion's share of work, take pains to be considerate about their preferences, feelings, and ideas. It's too easy to get tunnel vision and unwittingly alienate a lot of people.

- **Sharing the burdens.** Finding ways to divide and conquer the load of helping your parent does more than lighten the weight on you. It makes others feel invested and involved, which feeds collaboration. Resist the temptation to handle everything on your own. Even if a sibling seems mostly useless to you, find a way they can contribute—researching an option, driving to medical appointments, spending extra quality time with your parent.

- **Patching tender spots.** If dealing with things so far has exposed raw or difficult parts of your relationships with other family members, keep trying to reconcile with them. Generally, "the more the merrier—or at least, the more on the same page, the more progress and peace there's likely to be.

Build Up Your Eldercare Knowledge and Skills

If you have children of your own, you probably remember all the knowledge and skills you had to develop as part of that role.

Similarly, helping your aging parent means that you'll have to develop the relevant knowledge and skills. That's not to infantilize aging parents or to suggest this is an exact role reversal—obviously, it's more complicated than that.

Still, a skill set is involved. Exactly what you'll need to learn will depend on your particular situation, but in general, here's what people helping an aging parent usually have to learn to address:

- Helping with daily life tasks.

- Managing common safety issues.

- Assisting with health issues and navigating the medical system.

- Addressing legal and financial issues.

- Addressing housing and looking into alternative housing

arrangement.

- Quality of life and helping your older parent thrive.

- Planning ahead for declines and emergencies.

- Managing relationships and family dynamics.

- Your own self-care and renegotiating what you will and won't do.

This is a lot and you won't be able to learn it overnight—instead, you'll be learning it as you go along.

But the more proactive you can be about equipping yourself to learn, the better.

We especially recommend putting some time into reading a few good books and looking for a good support group, either locally or online.

(To help people like you get this kind of information, education, and support they need at this juncture, Dr. Kernisan created special online Helping Older Parents courses and programs. You can learn more in RESOURCES.)

Anticipate Emergencies and Future Declines

While you can't plan for every eventuality, once you have a handle on the current situation, you can train yourself to peer a little farther down the road.

The temptation is to avoid this and to just deal with things as they come up. The reality is that things ARE going to come up. Your parent will get sick, or fall, or require hospitalization. They won't be able to continue driving or manage their money. Their home will be too much for them to take care of or the stairs will be unnavigable. Some people will escape some of these scenarios, of course, but almost no one will escape all of them.

Now that you've started this journey with them, how will you navigate the inevitable bumps in the road?

You can't know the particulars. But you can begin to do the following:

- **Start "what if" conversations.** Involve your parent as best you can. Where would you like to live if you have to move from here? What if Dad can't drive any more, what would that look like? What if Mom has a relapse of her cancer?

- **Think about what possible future situations might look like.** Think about where your parent would live, who would provide what kind of care. Definitely keep talking among your siblings. Begin to research options to have in your back pocket as you need them.

- **Try to get a sense from your parent's doctor(s) about the likely trajectory of their conditions.** Are there specific things you can prepare for in terms of mobility or the type of care needed? What are typical complications you might expect?

- **Get your parent to designate surrogate decision makers if that hasn't happened yet.** If they're open to it, try to continue conversations that will guide you on how to make choices on their behalf. As uncomfortable as it may feel to bring up, your parent—or the partner who doesn't have cognitive impairment—may be willing to discuss advance care planning. (See RESOURCES.)

Keep Perspective

Helping your older parent journey through this phase of life is a huge role whether you've undertaken it willingly or not.

Throughout, remember this: **It's not your job to make everything perfect—or even better—for your parent.** As we've seen, those goals are often just not possible no matter what you do.

Your responsibility is to care and to make a good effort to help.

And if you spend even a little time applying what you've learned in this book, that's exactly what you'll have done: cared and made a good effort to help.

Resources

Downloadable Cheatsheets

The following printable cheatsheets can be downloaded for free from this book's online resource center.

Just visit Betterhealthwhileaging.net/book-bonuses

COGNITIVE SYMPTOM CHECKER

includes:

Concerning behaviors and symptoms

Brief description of symptoms

LIFE SKILLS & SAFETY PROBLEMS CHECKER

includes:

5 major areas of well-being to assess

Concerns to look for

HOW TO SAY IT: COMMUNICATING BETTER WITH YOUR PARENT WHEN YOU HAVE CONCERNS

includes:

Helpful things to say to gather information and avoid conflict

What NOT to say (especially when there is cognitive change)

WHAT HEALTH PROVIDERS SHOULD CHECK WHEN ASSESSING AN OLDER PERSON FOR COGNITIVE IMPAIRMENT

includes:

10 causes of cognitive impairment in older adults

10 things the doctor should do when evaluating cognitive impairment in an older adult

WHAT TO BRING TO A COGNITIVE/DEMENTIA EVALUATION

includes:

Information to gather before an appointment

What to be prepared to say

IS IT DEMENTIA? THE 5 KEY THINGS A DOCTOR IS LOOKING FOR TO MAKE A DIAGNOSIS

What providers consider as they make an evaluation

HOW TO PROMOTE BRAIN HEALTH & EMOTIONAL HEALTH

includes:

Recommended actions

Where to find out more

THE A-B-C WAY: A PROCESS FOR PICKING YOUR NEXT STEPS, AND TRYING THEM

includes:

The 6 basic steps to taking effective action

Worksheet space

Relevant Articles from
Dr. K's Better Health While Aging Website

HOW WE DIAGNOSE DEMENTIA: THE POPULAR BASICS TO KNOW

betterhealthwhileaging.net/how-to-diagnose-dementia-the-basics/

HOW MEMORY AND THINKING CHANGE WITH NORMAL AGING

betterhealthwhileaging.net/how-brain-function-changes-with-normal-cognitive-aging/

COMMON CAUSES OF COGNITIVE IMPAIRMENT

betterhealthwhileaging.net/cognitive-impairment-causes-and-how-to-evaluate/

MEDICATIONS KNOWN TO IMPAIR BRAIN FUNCTION

betterhealthwhileaging.net/medications-to-avoid-if-worried-about-memory/

HOW TO PROMOTE BRAIN HEALTH

betterhealthwhileaging.net/brain-health-checklist-8-proven-things-healthy-aging/)

FINANCIAL EXPLOITATION IN AGING: WHAT TO KNOW AND WHAT TO DO

betterhealthwhileaging.net/financial-abuse-what-to-know/

4 TYPES OF BRAIN-SLOWING MEDICATION TO AVOID IF YOU'RE WORRIED ABOUT MEMORY

betterhealthwhileaging.net/medications-to-avoid-if-worried-about-memory/

10 THINGS TO KNOW ABOUT HIPAA AND ACCESS TO A RELATIVE'S HEALTH INFORMATION

betterhealthwhileaging.net/hipaa-basics-and-faqs-for-family-caregivers/

INTERVIEW: REDUCING THE RISK OF POWER OF ATTORNEY ABUSE (PODCAST)

betterhealthwhileaging.net/podcast/bhwa/reduce-risk-power-of-attorney-abuse-david-godfrey/

7 STEPS TO MANAGING DIFFICULT DEMENTIA BEHAVIORS (SAFELY & WITHOUT MEDICATIONS)

betterhealthwhileaging.net/how-to-manage-difficult-alzheimers-behaviors-without-drugs/

Recommended Websites and References

FOR BROAD-BASED HELP

Better Health While Aging

Betterhealthwhileaging.net

Dr. K's comprehensive site provides practical articles, podcast episodes, and resources on how to address many common health problems that affect older adults. She also regularly covers common concerns and dilemmas related to helping older parents and other aging relatives.

Helping Older Parents Online Courses and Programs

Betterhealthwhileaging.net/helping-older-parents/

Dr. K created her original Helping Older Parents Bootcamp to coach adult children on how to effectively address the most common challenges that come up when assisting a declining aging parent. She continues to create and offer online courses and programs to support people helping aging parents, and to provide affordable access to experts such as herself and professional geriatric care managers.

Aging Life Care Association

aginglifecare.org

To learn more about and access a directory of geriatric care managers (the former but still-used name for what are now called aging life care professionals).

Administration on Aging's Eldercare Locator

Eldercare.acl.gov

Enter your zip code to find your local Area Agency on Aging as well as other local governmental resources on many aspects of older-adult life.

Family Caregiver Alliance

Caregiver.org

Along with a host of resources and educational materials for family caregivers, this longtime nonprofit's Family Care Navigator can help you access services near you.

Health in Aging

Healthinaging.org

The consumer-facing website of the American Geriatrics Society. See the useful section on medications for older adults.

National Elder Law Foundation

Nelf.org

This is the only national organization certifying practitioners of elder and special needs law, NELF's Certified Elder Law Attorney designation is itself certified by the American Bar Association. Includes a feature to help you find a certified elder law attorney.

National Academy of Elder Law Attorneys

Naela.org

This is a larger community of attorneys practicing elder law; includes a directory.

AARP Family Caregiving

Aarp.org/caregiving

Articles and tools in a special section of the organization's website.

Zen Caregiving Project

Zencaregiving.org

This group teaches mindfulness-based approaches and tools to help families and others manage emotional strain and support those in their care.

Powerful Tools for Caregivers

Powerfultoolsforcaregivers.org

A highly acclaimed program that teaches skills that can help reduce your stress and frustration

TO HELP ADDRESS MEMORY AND DEMENTIA CONCERNS

National Institute on Aging: What is Dementia? Symptoms, Types, and Diagnosis

Nia.nih.gov/health/what-dementia-symptoms-types-and-diagnosis

A helpful article explaining different types of dementia, including Alzheimer's disease and others.

Alzheimer's Association

Alz.org

The first national group focusing on awareness and research offers many general resources online and locally. Note that many areas have similar, just-as-terrific nonprofits doing similar work, such has CaringKind (New York City), Alzheimer's Texas, Alzheimer's Orange County (California), and Dementia Together (Northern Colorado).

Family Caregiver Alliance: Dementia Resources

Caregiver.org/health-issues/dementia

This nonprofit's general and topic-specific guides are especially thorough.

Dementia Map

Dementiamap.com

A new directory of companies, service providers, and other resources supporting the dementia community founded by the creators of two other helpful resources, Alzheimer's Speaks Radio and the Memory Café Directory, which includes more than 1,000 programs offering social outings for people with dementia.

TO HELP ADDRESS DRIVING CONCERNS

Drivers 65+

Seniordriving.aaa.com/wp-content/uploads/2016/08/Driver652.pdf

An online self-evaluation from the AAA Foundation for Traffic Safety.

American Occupational Therapy Association

Aota.org

Features a database of OTs who conduct driving evaluations.

AARP Driver Safety: We Need to Talk

Aarp.org/auto/driver-safety/we-need-to-talk

A free, self-paced online seminar created by The Hartford and the MIT AgeLab to help you determine how to assess someone's driving skills and to give you tools to have this important conversation.

National Highway Traffic Safety Administration: Older Drivers

Nhtsa.gov/road-safety/older-drivers

This comprehensive guide includes advice on influencing older drivers, a link to state laws pertaining to driver licensing requirements, and other resources.

National Institute on Aging: Driving Safety and Alzheimer's Disease

Nia.nih.gov/health/driving-safety-and-alzheimers-disease

Added information for when there are cognitive concerns.

TO HELP SAFEGUARD FINANCES

Better Health While Aging: Financial Exploitation in Aging—What to Know and What to Do

Betterhealthwhileaging.net/financial-abuse-what-to-know

How to know if someone is at risk and what to do.

Consumer Reports: What to Do When You Suspect Financial Abuse

Consumerreports.org/cro/magazine/2013/01/protecting-mom-dad-s-money

This well-written article includes common financial abuse scenarios, suggestions of what to do, and a good list of additional online resources.

National Council on Aging: Top 10 Financial Scams Targeting Seniors

Ncoa.org/economic-security/money-management/scams-security/top-10-scams-targeting-seniors

This list can help you become more aware of what to watch for.

TO HELP REDUCE HOME HAZARDS

University of Buffalo Home Safety Self-Assessment Tool

Sphhp.buffalo.edu/rehabilitation-science/research-and-facilities/fund-ed-research/aging/home-safety-self-assessment-tool.html

CDC: Check for Safety: A Home Fall Prevention Checklist

Cdc.gov/HomeandRecreationalSafety/pubs/English/booklet_Eng_desktop-a.pdf

AARP HomeFit Guide

Aarp.org/livable-communities/housing/info-2020/homefit-guide

For advice on helping someone age in place safely.

TO LEARN MORE ABOUT HIPAA

HHS.gov: HIPAA rules

Hhs.gov/hipaa/for-professionals/faq/index.html

Search "provider share information" for specifics relevant to doctors and family members.

TO LEARN MORE ABOUT END-OF-LIFE PLANNING DISCUS-SIONS

The Conversation Project

Theconversationproject.org

Prepare For Your Care

Prepareforyourcare.org

AARP: Starting the Conversation About End-of-Life Care

Aarp.org/caregiving/basics/info-2020/end-of-life-talk-care-talk/

Recommended Reads

The Caregiver's Encyclopedia: A Compassionate Guide to Caring for Older Adults by Muriel R. Gillick, MD
Comprehensive guidance from a geriatrician about how to manage caregiving and decision-making, from doctor visits to hospitalizations, rehab, chronic and acute care at home, and nursing home care.

How to Care for Aging Parents: A One-Stop Resource for all your Medical, Financial, Housing, and Emotional Issues by Virginia Morris
An encyclopedic classic on medical, financial, housing, and emotional issues related to helping an older parent.

Surviving Alzheimer's: Practical Tips and Soul-Saving Wisdom for Caregivers by Paula Spencer Scott
A comprehensive guide to helping someone with dementia, featuring situation-specific advice, special emphasis on family dynamics and self-care, and insights leading experts including Dr. K, educator Teepa Snow, Alzheimer's Association cofounder Lisa Gwyther, neurologist Richard Isaacson, advocate Leeza Gibbons, and others.

The Parent Care Conversation: 6 Strategies for Dealing With the Emotional and Financial Challenges of Aging Parents by Dan Taylor
Suggestions for discussing money, property, home, professional care, and more with empathy and success.

Navigating Your Later Years for Dummies by Carol Levine
An AARP-branded guide, by the author of Planning for Long-Term Care for Dummies (both part of the *Dummies* series) including guidance on home modification, sources of care, legal documents, and more.

Juggling Life, Work, and Caregiving by Amy Goyer
Another AARP guide that specifically addresses the needs of those who are holding down jobs while helping parents, especially over the long-haul.

Acknowledgements

Above all, this book is a direct outcome of my experiences over the years with countless older adults and families that I've had the privilege to help in person, and also with the even greater number of people I've interacted with online, through questions posted to the Better Health While Aging website and through my interactive online workshops and courses. I'm particular grateful to the first members of the Helping Older Parents Bootcamp and to those who have been part of our other online programs. These encounters directly shaped my approach to effectively and compassionately supporting an aging adult who needs our help. This can be fraught stuff! To that end, I'm deeply grateful to each individual who has shared a part of their journey with me, and to everyone who has encouraged me in this work.

Extra special thanks to the ever-thoughtful Linda Fodrini-Johnson, geriatric care manager extraordinaire, who has been a colleague and mentor to me for many years. She was the first reader of this book's manuscript and provided much good feedback that found its way into these pages.

— L.K.

About the Authors

LESLIE KERNISAN, MD, MPH, is a practicing geriatrician and the founder of the popular aging health website and podcast Better Health While Aging, which she created to help families and older adults learn better ways to manage common aging health challenges. "Dr. K" has a special interest in helping families of aging adults through online programs, to enable more people to access the expertise of geriatricians. She currently offers a Helping Older Parents Course and other online programs to provide expert guidance to people caring for aging parents. She's also a clinical instructor at the University of California, San Francisco, Division of Geriatrics. Previously, the site medical director of the Over 60 Health Clinic in Berkeley and the founder of the Geri-Tech blog, her first book was Better Digital Health for Aging, an industry guide. She trained in internal medicine and geriatrics at UCSF and is a proud graduate of Princeton University and Case Western Reserve School of Medicine. She lives in San Francisco.

See betterhealthwhileaging.net

PAULA SPENCER SCOTT is an award-winning writer on health and aging and the author of more than a dozen books, including *Surviving Alzheimer's: Practical Tips and Soul-Saving Wisdom for Caregivers* and collaborations with doctors at Harvard, UCLA, and Duke. A journalist fellow of the Gerontological Society of America, her work appears in Parade, PBS Next Avenue, AARP, and other national media. She also gives talks on caregiver support and brain health. She lives in Colorado.

See paulaspencerscott.com

CPSIA information can be obtained
at www.ICGtesting.com
Printed in the USA
LVHW020152230721
693426LV00013B/1265